Forgotten Memories

Forgotten Memories

A JOURNEY OUT OF
THE DARKNESS
OF SEXUAL ABUSE

Barbara Schave

Foreword by Douglas Schave

PRAEGER

Westport, Connecticut
London

Library of Congress Cataloging-in-Publication Data

Schave, Barbara.
    Forgotten memories : a journey out of the darkness of sexual abuse /
Barbara Schave ; foreword by Douglas Schave.
        p.   cm.
    Includes bibliographical references and index.
    ISBN 0–275–94542–1
    1. Schave, Barbara—Mental health.   2. Adult child sexual abuse
victims—United States—Biography.   3. Psychotherapy patients—
United States—Biography.   I. Title.
RC569.5.A28S33   1993
616.85'82239'0092—dc20   93–6773
[B]

British Library Cataloguing in Publication Data is available.

Library of Congress Catalog Card Number: 93–6773
ISBN: 0–275–94542–1

First published in 1993

Praeger Publishers, 88 Post Road West, Westport, CT   06881
An imprint of Greenwood Publishing Group, Inc.

Printed in the United States of America

The paper used in this book complies with the
Permanent Paper Standard issued by the National
Information Standards Organization (Z39.48–1984).

10 9 8 7 6 5 4 3 2 1

To the memory of My Mother

To Arnold W. Wilson
Douglas, Richard and Elizabeth Schave
Marjorie and Jon Ford:

For their wisdom, humanity and
courage as my guides
on this inner journey

Contents

Foreword

Douglas Schave, M.D.

Writing the foreword on a story that has so powerfully affected me personally is difficult. The story is a very painful one and, without the benefit of my wife's second analyst, would also have been a very tragic one.

Abuse of any kind is wrong. The abuse of a child is worse than the abuse of an adult. Unlike an adult, a child cannot walk out of an abusive relationship. Children are totally dependent on the very people who are abusing them—they are trapped.

Sexual abuse, however, is by far the most tragic experience for a child. As stated quite bluntly by R. Frederickson (1992), sexual abuse is far more damaging than any other type of abuse because of the secrecy surrounding it and the resulting sense of total isolation. Physical and emotional abuse of one or several family members takes place in "public," whether in front of all the family members or out in a public space. Even young children can see that these forms of abuse are not right. Children growing up in an abusive environment may expect abuse; they may even have to deny their reality and accept it, but on some level they know that not all families act abusively. Sexual abuse, perpetrated in private, is totally isolating and thus much more insidious and damaging psychologically and emotionally. There is no audience and no one available to make comparisons.

Adults who abuse their children often tell them that they love them. How can young children defend themselves against such a statement? To survive psychologically, an abused child, especially a gifted child, must rationalize the situation. The child does so by thinking, "They must love me, so this is good for me. They wouldn't hurt me intentionally. They are trying as hard as they can to be good." Oftentimes adults threaten children with horror stories—with being killed or skinned alive—or they show brutal acts on animals as a warning not to tell anyone. A child thus threatened is totally alone, figuratively, and at times literally, stripped naked and totally vulnerable.

In this total aloneness and extreme vulnerability the evils of shame come into play. Often from birth, children who are abused are treated as less than human. The adult's contempt toward the child, the belittlement and its resultant sense of being subhuman, of being a defective human being, is directly and indirectly transmitted to the infant or child. When the infant reaches toddlerhood, the consolidation of its cognitive phase, preoperational thinking, results in the formation of a dynamic unconscious. With this consolidation, the sense of defectiveness and ensuing shame, humiliation, mortification, and so on, becomes an integral part of the youngster's unconscious. Unless exposed and worked through in intensive psychoanalytically oriented psychotherapy or psychoanalysis, this sense of defectiveness and shame festers, causing a lifelong undermining of that individual's positive sense of self-worth and self-esteem.

For the gifted and exceptionally gifted child, this dynamic can be even more powerful and destructive. Gifted infants, already taking in massive amounts of information at a much earlier age than most infants and children, organize information as if they are the center of the universe. They explain what happens in the world based on what they do, think, or say— or don't do, don't think, or don't say. As a result, often children between two and six feel they are responsible for everything.

When a parent abuses a child, especially a gifted child, the child feels that he or she, not the parent or adult, has done something wrong. This notion of being wrong intensifies the sense of shame and, unfortunately, also increases their isolation. Sexually abused children are left to fend for themselves. There is no protection; there is no help. Adults cannot be trusted. But one cannot live in a world in which one constantly feels so threatened. To survive, children must first shut off their feelings and then become what the adult needs them to be. As a result, abused children disconnect from their feelings through disavowal, disassociation, and denial. Once the feelings are buried, then the second barrier of repression buries the memories. Thus the abused can now live in the abusive environment with the perpetrators of the crime, but they do so at enormous cost to their emotional life, for they live with "forgotten memories."

While this is a story of my wife struggling with her lifelong sense of shame and isolation from being sexually abused, this story is also becoming more prominent with males. One of my recent analytic patients had seen several therapists who never even suspected that he had been sexually abused by his mother. Yet after several years of analytic work, he gradually remembered an image of his mother's face looking down at him with a loving smile. The smiling face remains for about a minute as he feels increasingly excited and sexually aroused. Suddenly the maternal smile turns into a panicked look and there is a sudden disconnection—her face disappears. At that moment, my patient experiences a terrifying sense of chaos and loss. His realization of being sexually abused as an infant helped him to understand years of sexualizing relationships.

The most tragic part of the victimization of children is that the cycle continues. Some families can be traced back generations in terms of the perpetuation of abuse. What is even more tragic, as in the case of my wife and many victims of sexual abuse, well-meaning and highly educated analysts do not even suspect a history of sexual abuse. In my wife's case, in retrospect, the clues were all there: avoiding talk about sexual issues, reporting discomfort when her own patients spoke about sexual matters, and facing her analyst's inability to accept, understand, and tolerate her feeling states. Progressing in her roles as wife, mother, and student, she made the assumption that all was going well in her treatment. Wrong!

The theories of classical Freudian analysts do not seem to allow for the investigation of poor self-esteem and issues of shame. As one instructor in my analytic training stated, "I really enjoy the struggle of the Oedipal period with my female patients. I don't like to mother them." There lies the problem with many analysts, often male. They don't want "to mother," which means that they don't want to work at the early emotional levels of their patients' injuries. For the traumas discussed in this book are from the earliest moments of life. Abused children suffer adults' contempt and disrespect from birth. The issues are not pre-Oedipal or even pregenital. The issues are developmental from the earliest period of life. These patients are dealing with feeling states and experiences that often have no words or meaning to them because they are preverbal. Often these patients lack the ability to symbolize, which creates a very concrete patient or at best a patient with a lack of memories or associations. Patients with such developmental arrests are not resistant or defiant patients but, rather, patients who were never helped to articulate early experiences and their accompanying feelings. Fortunately, Dr. Ace was one analyst who was not afraid to enter that earliest period of childhood with all of its terrors and boogie-men. For my wife, myself, and our family, we are grateful.

When one does not feel understood in one's psychotherapy, particularly psychoanalysis, one feels totally alone. In that terrible sense of isolation and aloneness is a revictimization and recreation of abuse. Such is the experience my wife had with her first analyst. This was in stark contrast with her experience with her second analyst. Dr. Ace's ability to "be there" emotionally with her allowed her not only to remember her forgotten memories but to reexperience and integrate these overwhelming feelings as a highly intelligent and well-functioning adult.

This book is her story, a story of how she was freed from the past and how she is no longer a victim of her forgotten memories.

Acknowledgments

Writing can be such a solitary experience. I was so very fortunate that I had so many family members, friends, and colleagues to keep me company as I worked on this manuscript. I am so grateful to them for their persistence and emotional support; their reactions were woven into the manuscript, and I believe that it is their feedback that gives my manuscript more meaning and warmth.

I will begin my thank you's at the beginning of the project. I am grateful to my mother, Sylvia Title, for giving me her courage, love, and her support. Although she passed away before this book was finished, she was deeply concerned that I tell my story—our story.

Next I thank Arnold W. Wilson, M.D., for agreeing to take me on as a patient at the end of a long, successful, and distinguished career. Dr. Wilson believed he could help me, and he did. I appreciate his generosity, his genuine warmth, kindness, and seriousness about what was in my best interest. His persistence and insight helped me to rewrite this manuscript from beginning to end.

I am very grateful to Peter Hancoff, my writer friend and soul mate, for helping me create the title *Forgotten Memories* when this book was just a vision in my mind.

I thank Judy Smith for typing the first draft of the manuscript. Her generosity started me on my mission to write about my forgotten memories.

Sidney Kramer, my literary agent, and his staff believed in my words and their meanings and their efforts sustained me as I tried to find a publisher for this manuscript. Sidney Kramer's calm manner and his serious sense of purpose helped me to mold the manuscript in a personal way. He encouraged me to stick with my vision.

I am so grateful for having an intelligent and wonderful husband, Douglas Schave, who took over Judy Smith's original draft and helped me to explain my ideas more clearly. Without his understanding and insight, I would not have sold the manuscript. My husband's untiring interest and spirit to complete this manuscript was a daily inspiration. At my request he typed every word I wrote and then retyped what I rewrote until I was satisfied that I was communicating my story. I know that I am extremely fortunate to have his support and love.

My sister, Marjorie Ford, became interested in my story, as you will come to understand when you read this book. Her empathy and unbeguiling, persistent concern for my well-being was untiring, and her memories gave this manuscript a dimension that only she could add.

I was fortunate that Paul Macirowski, Psychology Editor at Praeger Publishers, believed that writing *Forgotten Memories* was the right decision, and I am thankful for his insights into the meaning of my words and their explication as I worked with him on this manuscript. I appreciate his sincerity and compassion for me as an author.

Finally, I thank my children, Richard and Elizabeth, for their continued inspiration, patience, warmth, sense of humor, and love, which allows me to write on.

Forgotten Memories

Prologue

This is a haunting story about the ghosts of childhood that live on in the darkness within us in spite of our own persistence to turn on the lights and to see these demons that lurk in hidden corners of our psyches. My story is a tale of despair, deep rage, and betrayal. Yet it is also a story of understanding myself and the traumatic abuse from which I suffered, of going on, and of finding hope for the future through a sense of rebirth.

My memories of incestuous experiences came back to me in a very powerful and confusing order. Because these experiences were rooted in deep shame and an enforced secrecy, I have attempted to reflect on the nature of the shame and secrecy in my writing style and the sequencing of the manuscript. This story unfolds in a way that parallels my own growing consciousness about being traumatically sexually abused. At first, my childhood demons came into my awareness gradually and unpredictably. My focus and understanding gradually become stronger and clearer and more forthright and disclosing as I become more emotionally connected with my experiences, and more able to believe and then tolerate these painful memories as I spoke about them and then as I wrote these words down.

I have chosen to maintain this unconventional style in a deliberate attempt to share with the reader the evolution of painful understandings of traumatic childhood events. I am attempting to explain that recalling painful events comes gradually as one begins to emotionally understand the importance of the courage to see and hold on to horrible and frightening truths.

ONE

The Calm before the Storm

I am an identical twin, although there were many years now in my past when I wished I could divest myself of this identity. I am also a wife and a mother of two grown children. Professionally, I am a clinical psychologist and the coauthor of several psychological texts. I have written this seemingly complicated and painful story in hope that this personal odyssey will be meaningful to individuals considering beginning psychoanalysis or intensive psychotherapy. I have also written this story because of my serious concern with the lack of knowledge about detection and treatment of childhood and sexual abuse. This book contributes my personal and professional understanding to other victims, their families, and their therapists.

I will explain "what went wrong," why my first analyst did not suspect sexual abuse or incest. Ostensibly, my first experience with psychoanalysis, by all superficial measures, should have been successful because I fulfilled all the criteria for an analysand. I am introspective, committed to understanding relationships, and capable of integrating painful understandings. In turn, my first analyst was highly trained and had an excellent reputation. He was a caring individual devoted to helping others. But in the end our work not only failed but was destructive

in that it recreated unconscious childhood traumas, which pre-
cipitated a very serious depression for me.

My first analyst never considered that I had been molested as
a child by my father and brother, in spite of all the struggles
and traumas I shared with him about my childhood. By communicating my experiences in analysis, both good and bad, I
hope the reader will better understand the subjective, highly
personal nature of the therapeutic bond, its value, and its limitations, as well as the difficulties in treating survivors of childhood sexual abuse.

*   *   *

Any type of abuse, but most especially childhood sexual
abuse, creates a deep sense of shame about oneself and engen-
ders a need to keep these feelings of shame secret. This sense
of shame and secrecy is experienced as a basic sense of being
defective—of not being worthy as a human being. Because of
the need to hide from this pervasive sense of shame, for many
years I had difficulty facing, let alone talking and then writing
about, what happened to me in my first analysis, let alone my
childhood. First of all, there is a serious taboo about incest in
our society. People don't openly talk about being sexually
abused. I have also gotten serious and critical feedback from my
friends and colleagues that talking about incest is an outrageous
thing to do, particularly if you are concerned about your professional identity. These personal reactions of significant others
have been confusing, overwhelming, hurtful, and even overly
empathic. It has been extremely hard to expose myself to indif-
ference or over-concern. On the other hand, I also feel outraged
that my role in society as a woman, that my feminine identity,
perpetuated my victimization. What happened to me makes me
wonder how victims of sexual abuse are able to become full,
functioning members of society. Having made it to the "other
side," I feel compelled to risk my privacy and my concern about
exposure and being misunderstood in order to help other people

become survivors rather than victims of incest or other types of sexual abuse.

I understand now how unconsciously taking care of my first analyst's emotional needs unknowingly recreated the trauma of my childhood. Sacrificing my emotional or personal needs for him reawakened deep feelings of shame and horror so terrifying that they were buried in a pervasive amnesia about my childhood. Only now, because I understand the source of my shame, is my sense of defectiveness less overwhelming. Only with the help of a supportive family, friends, and a new, wiser, and kinder analyst have I developed enough distance from my shame and anger to describe my experience without feeling desperately hopeless about the usefulness of therapeutic relationships. It has been a long, personal journey to get to a place where I feel able to trust that my feelings are important and meaningful to me and to others. Through my experiences with my second analyst I learned about the importance of my own feelings and inclinations. Now I believe that understanding a patient's feelings and their emotional source is the only way to help that patient develop a sense of self-worth and to recover from feeling ashamed and defective.

I hope that my experiences will open up new ways to look at and understand childhood sexual abuse and also to prevent and protect others from experiencing the terror and traumas of being first sexually abused as a child and then emotionally exploited by a therapist or analyst. B. Noël and K. Watterson (1992) have also written of a similar personal experience of the sexual revictimization of a sexually abused patient by her analyst. I am sure that I am not alone in feeling betrayed by an analyst.

As difficult and painful as this sad story is to tell, I want to illustrate the potential power and potential destructiveness of the therapeutic bond. For me, analysis was more than just an experience that fits into a category that has been described in the psychological/psychoanalytic literature as a negative therapeutic encounter or a treatment failure. For me, psychoanalysis became a trip into the dark pit of nothingness. With the help of my new analyst, I ascended from hell, a hell that I had always assumed was what life was all about.

I will begin this story in the middle, rather than the beginning. I will jump back and forth in time, from past to present and back to the present, in order to illustrate how psychoanalysis or intensive psychoanalytic psychotherapy, which sets out to be curative, was for me ultimately devastating and destructive.

My focus throughout this book is on the therapeutic bond and how it can be used to detect sexual abuse or other forms of early traumatic abuse. An interactive and interpersonal connection between patient and psychotherapist, the therapeutic bond is an emotional, intellectual, physical, and nonverbal link or connection between two people who work intensely together. Their work is to understand the patient's past experiences, whether remembered, repressed, or totally forgotten, for these experiences contribute to the patient's present way of perceiving and interacting with the world of people and things. The therapeutic bond is comprised of the real feelings the therapist and patient have toward each other, as well as the fantasies or expectations both bring to the relationship from their own lives, especially their childhood.

My awareness that my relationship, or bond, with my analyst was troubled became conscious during my training as a clinical psychologist. Only as I began to work with patients did I become increasingly aware that something was drastically wrong in my own analysis. Only then did I realize the profound impact the therapeutic bond can have on another human being. I began to understand the bond between patient and therapist from an entirely different perspective. As a patient in psychoanalysis, I had only a few basic preconceptions about what to expect from my psychoanalysis, the work of understanding my childhood. Clearly, I accepted that I would understand more accurately my own history and its effects on my life choices. I entered this relationship expecting to get help in becoming a more enlightened and insightful person. Specifically, I thought that I would understand how my twinship affected my way of relating to the

world. I believed that my doctor could and would help me un-
cover the significant roots in, or emotional links to, my past. My
belief in psychoanalysis was supported by significant others
around me, especially my husband, who was then just entering
the field of psychiatry, and our close friends. Perhaps I was
intellectually naive in expecting this reputable doctor to help
me, holding my own best interests at the heart of his work, our
work. Emotionally, I had very few personal resources to assess
whether I was being treated fairly.

I thought, again perhaps blindly and foolishly, that my doctor
was objective about what would be understood to be in my own
best interests. In other words, I thought that he would know
how to "cure" me or at least help me with my insecurities,
anxieties, and unhappiness. I believed he would put my interests
and needs ahead of his conscious or unconscious personal needs;
never did I consider that he had his own agenda. I was paying
for a service, I thought, and in return I would get treatment. At
first I did not suspect that he was asking for more than payment
for services rendered—that he also expected me "to perform"
in a certain fashion. I believed that the essence of the therapeutic
bond was that my emotional needs as the patient would come
first. I thought that primary to the work was the patient's
agenda, not the analyst's sense of how things should proceed.
Because of my own repressive and abusive childhood experiences, I did not question my analyst's agenda, nor his motiva-
tions, nor, more importantly, his limitations. Because I did not
question his skill and integrity, I became his analytic victim. The
sad, regretful truth is that my first analyst has no capacity nor
desire to comprehend why I am enraged with him. His own
denial system protects him too tenaciously. I know this now.
But then, as a young woman, I was vulnerable to his mistreat-
ment and ultimately to his unconscious exploitation of my feelings. Thinking about this enrages me. I cannot stop thinking
about this problem, for who should be accountable to the patient,
if not the doctor? Can this curse of the soul and spirit be prevented? How can truly deep-rooted issues in an individ-

ual's life be uncovered and addressed? This crucial problem is, as I now know, even more serious with victims of sexual abuse because on a very deep level they feel they must hold on to their secret and their shame "against all odds."

*   *   *

As a beginning psychotherapist, I "connected well" with my patients emotionally. They liked me or found me engaging, and they felt safe with me. It struck me in a very profound way that I could help make a situation, an interpersonal experience, or interaction better or worse for another person based on my evaluation of what would be helpful. I could help patients understand themselves and/or I could make mistakes and hurt my patients' self-development based on my assessment of what they needed or didn't need—on how they reacted or didn't react to my point of view. Patients were clearly vulnerable to my sense of what was in their own best interest, whether it be understanding, insight, advice, or just listening. Whether or not I was saying or doing the right thing, that is, acting in the patient's behalf, I was clearly important to my patients' sense of themselves.

Gaining a sense of myself as a therapist was an enormous as well as a very gradual and difficult task due to the complexity of understanding the therapeutic process. While in training I was highly motivated to be the best therapist I could be. I was driven to understand why people had emotional problems and how to help them. My understanding involved hands-on experience with patients, consultation with supervisors and peers, and reading the literature on psychoanalysis and psychotherapy. This was a truly intense and compelling process. Being in training is a strange experience because the search for truthfulness and accuracy is extremely important, which is often not the reality when you are in private practice or working on the staff of a clinic or hospital. I was encouraged to move from one set of therapeutic circumstances and situations to the next, continually concerned about my approach to the patients.

When my training was over, I was no longer answerable to my supervisors for my actions and reactions as a therapist. My new independence and power felt strange. Truthfulness and accuracy were put on the back burner as I faced the reality of keeping my practice alive, let alone theoretically correct. Theoretically as well as practically, this is a big switch and an important one for a therapist. Indeed, accountability toward patients may be the turning point for some therapists. I know I still kept my sense of responsibility to my patients' inner life and experience, although responsibility to the patient was definitely different from accountability to a supervisor for what I was trying to accomplish in my own office with my patients.

* * *

As completion of my long years of training approached, I found an office in a desirable location. I was delighted to have a place to call my own after years of sharing and switching offices with fellow trainees. I was ready to serve the world, eager to work therapeutically with my first private patients. In that very first month alone, in my office, I had an experience I will never forget. One bright morning Lori, a young movie actress, walked into the office and cheerfully said, "Is this going to be a 'take'?" Immediately and spontaneously I answered yes, though at the moment I wasn't sure about what she was asking me to give to her. I have gone over this incident many times in my mind. Why did I say yes? Other therapists might have pondered, "What does 'a take' mean to you?" or "What are you feeling when you ask me this?" Some therapists might have said, in a more or less direct way, "This is not a movie set!" and then explained the purpose of the therapeutic process. But I intuitively said yes. My spontaneity was extremely important in my developing a rapport with this young woman. On later reflection I believed that she wanted to know that I could tolerate and accept her feelings. My capacity to understand that she also needed my hopefulness, rather than an interpretation of her state of mind or behavior at that moment, has been crucial to this young woman's capacity to understand her inner experiences and to function in her own behalf in her life and in our work together.

In thinking back on my formal training, I believe that my experiences as a daughter, sister, mother, wife, graduate student, and patient in psychoanalysis have all had a significant impact on my development as a clinical psychologist. These extracurricular roles were just as significant as all 12 years of my formal training and supervision. In other words, by the end of the period of my formal training in clinical psychology, I was ready for this therapeutic encounter with Lori. Working with Lori was crucial in my finally realizing the problems that were going on in my first analysis and the trauma of my own childhood. I think that Lori seriously challenged my sense of the comparative value and limitations of confrontation, judgments, advice, and the need for understanding as crucial parts of the therapeutic process.

Working with Lori, I came upon a fundamental truth about the therapeutic relationship. Stated simply, when therapists understand themselves better, they understand the patient better. I learned from my young patient a truth about my own life by understanding my reactions to the experiences she described to me.

I remember thinking during my first session with Lori, sitting in my small office at the training hospital where I worked, "What a beautiful and intriguing young woman." Beyond her intense pain, with which I sensed she was struggling, I saw enormous courage and a strong belief that she could make her life more understandable. I sensed, along with her ability for introspection, a longing for understanding and insight into her troubled life. Only later, as we delved into her past, did she experience feelings of being totally overwhelmed and of being terrified of the world. At those moments she required direct and concrete interventions. Her fluctuating capacity to cope with her life stresses and her changing emotional states of mind were not the theme of the beginning of our work together, however. In fact, it took us three years of working together before she was able to talk about sometimes feeling in control and other times feeling quite fragile and out of control. At those moments I was proud of her for having the courage to experience and confront these intense feelings. I often reflected on my initial impression of her, which had been that at times she seemed like a fragile piece of porcelain that needed to be handled with extremely delicate care. And yet these episodes were interspersed with other times when she showed courage and a capacity for problem solving that had allowed her to survive, to cope with her stressful and challenging life. Such immediate bonding as that between Lori and me, and the ability to understand another person so quickly and deeply, is not usually the case. Unconsciously I identified myself with Lori. I also took my role in her life very seriously, becoming deeply concerned with my reactions to her pain and to her courage. My convictions about helping Lori were extremely meaningful for both of us.

*   *   *

I have come to believe strongly that it is the therapist's responsibility to be concerned about what he or she contributes to the patient's well-being and psychological growth because analysts or therapists cannot really be objective (Kohut, 1977, 1984; Stolorow & Atwood, 1987). All helping professionals are biased by their own expectations for themselves and their patients. The more aware therapists are of their own reactions, called countertransference, the more useful the therapeutic experience will be for the patient, and in turn, the more effective the therapeutic experience will be for the therapist. Unfortunately, it is often far too threatening for therapists to be honest about their own reactions to their patients.

My first analyst thought that he was objective, neutral, and always accurate in his interpretations. If I interviewed him today, he would say that I am exaggerating his mistakes. I speculate that because of his personality structure he would blame me for "not working harder." I imagine that he would say, in his own folksy way, that we accomplished an enormous amount in our work together. He would point out that I obtained two doctorates, published three books, remained married, and raised two children who are well-functioning. Our work, in his mind, was a resounding success. He is proud of our work, or perhaps I should say he is proud of his work. Superficially, he is correct. He did a terrific job as a career counselor. But he failed as an analyst because over many years of hard work I was never able to get in touch with my early emotional memories, which would have allowed me to develop a truer sense of myself and in turn diminish my feelings of defectiveness. Although intellectually I came to understand my role in the family, my emotional experiences as a child were not explored. I came to realize that I was treated like the bad twin—the family scapegoat, the bad seed. But why was I treated as the bad one? And why was this one interpretation so crucial? Why didn't my first analyst encourage me to question him? And why was I so ready to accept his point of view and advice? Although my first analyst realized that we had not dealt with the negative transference (my anger at him), he was not concerned enough or did not see it as important enough to explore my anger and fear of him as well as other men in my life. We never explored the emotional meanings of my role growing up in my family. Perhaps he unconsciously believed he could not handle his reactions to the feelings and thoughts I had repressed. I hold him responsible for not being able to tolerate my feelings. I hold him responsible for not working through his own feelings about me and his daughter's death so that I could have shared my feelings and fears rather than keep them hidden. I believe now that because of his own personal reasons, limitations, and need for control, he saw me as a fragile child—a message he transmitted to me both directly and unconsciously. Had he been less afraid of his own feelings and fear of closeness, would he have wondered about why he needed to see me as someone in need of protection who could not survive on her own? Why did he focus on my fragilities rather than on my courage to face them? Why was he so afraid of my feelings? Did he know his fear would cause me to hide my feelings from myself as well as from him? Did he do this consciously or unconsciously so that he would not have to struggle with his own fears and limitations? I would say yes to these questions. He would say no.

I know I will never have concrete answers to these provocative and troublesome questions from a black and white legal standpoint. However, I do know that I began to think seriously about these issues when my young actress patient began therapy with me. I worked very hard to foster a sense of protection for my young patient. I encouraged her to develop a sense of safety with me, while at the same time helping her to feel that she could also get through troublesome and emotional experiences on her own. I tried to give her the right amount of protection— not too much, not too little. This is, I came to realize, what I had needed for myself in my first analysis. I wanted to understand what was underneath her driven behavior and to help her understand herself. I wanted to provide a safe enough place for her to become aware of her feelings and to get in touch with and reconstruct her memories. I did not need to judge her competence as an adult nor help her make decisions for her life choices and her career.

*   *   *

With hindsight, life is always more understandable. I feel pleased that I can now put this enraging and disappointing experience in perspective and write about it. I wonder, am I enraged just by my first analyst or am I enraged by all the Freudian-trained analysts in the city and by Sigmund Freud himself, who couched his ideas and theories in metaphors about fantasized incest when he knew that some fathers were seducing their daughters? Was Freud afraid to be too provocative, so he made up the Oedipal conflict because he thought people would listen to this theory of development more readily? Freud's deceit has been cruelly harmful to too many sexually abused women (Masson, 1984, 1991).

On a more personal level, I was at first also angry at everyone who could have helped me see what was happening. Sometimes I am angry at myself for not knowing then what I know now. For as I think about my own work in my first analysis as a young woman, I now see clearly that I was blinded and vulnerable because I was uneducated about what to expect and I was un-knowingly victimized, unable to protect myself. Unfortunately, my lack of expectations also hurt my husband, my children, my mother, and my twin sister. We all became trapped in my ideal-ization of my analyst, who allowed himself to be elevated to godlike stature. When problems came up, my husband and I turned to him for answers. He encouraged this stance. He did not want to believe that I could solve my own problems, and he did not encourage me to try, even though I had always been able to carry on with my life. Instead, he needed to solve what he believed to be my problems for me, leaving me feeling not only helpless and fragile but isolated and worthless. As a result of his expectations and perspectives, I became driven to achieve success, but I was unable to feel good about my accomplish-ments. Whose achievements were they anyway? Who was I working for? When I was not working for someone else, I felt so alone that it seemed unbearable. At times it was truly fright-ening to have nothing to do.

In short, instead of feeling better about myself as a competent adult, I came to feel that my judgments were always lacking something. I always felt defective. I needed far too much affir-mation from others. Trusting my own sense of the situation felt dangerous because I felt so inadequate. In addition, when I was alone and not working for others, my life felt frighteningly empty. I felt like a fraud. I shudder writing this down. I feel sick to my stomach—what a traumatic experience! Clearly, my first analysis reactivated or recreated my childhood experiences that were so traumatically injurious. As a child I was made to feel that I was responsible for other people's happiness and that I could never do enough of whatever was asked of me, including sexual intimacies. When I terminated my first analysis, the conflicts and struggles I had felt when I first began my analysis intensified. My treatment had been but an enactment of my familial role as all-purpose caregiver.

* * *

This book tells the story of my own painful enlightenment about the difficulty of getting psychological treatment if you are the survivor of sexual abuse. But it also tells the story of getting help in psychoanalysis and about the healing process of knowing the truth and learning to act on your own behalf.

TWO

Addressing My Sense of Despair

Reflecting on the reality that you are *alone* in making your own decisions about life can be challenging, exciting, and/or scary if you are honest with yourself. And depending on your personality, this is more or less a conscious consideration. For example, some people consciously give up their authority to another individual, a god or a deity, or even a set of theoretical beliefs. Other people consciously as well as unconsciously give up their authority, power, or decision making to their personal insecurities or their fantasies of power, omnipotence, and grandiosity. Or narcissistic injuries—that is, self-perceptions based on unresolved painful shame—limit the range of the individual's capacity to experience life. In other words, because of their distinct psychological histories, individuals react in understandable ways to their own life experiences; this reaction affects their capacity to act in their own best interests and to make an impact on others. In some sense we are all victims or survivors of our past.

Children who have been valued by their parents and given choices about their life decisions are much more likely to be able to take charge of their lives as adults. But children who have taken care of their parents at the expense of their own self-development are definitely unprepared to make decisions on their own behalf. Children without ample or adequate parenting in childhood grow up with a diminished ability to know what they want and need from others, and they are vulnerable to being used or exploited by others.

Children who have been victims of sexual abuse have their own particular way of dealing with this serious trauma to their psyche and the resulting distortion in the development of their sense of self. The shame and humiliation and the need for secrecy that they experience is so intense and frightening that they are, in most instances, unable to talk about their feelings of shame and pain without professional help. Repression, disassociation, disavowal, denial, and amnesia are very common reactions to sexual abuse, making it difficult, if not impossible, for the victim to be aware of the actual traumatic events. Victims of sexual abuse are essentially completely alone with their traumatic experience until they unlock secrets deep inside their souls. Uncovering these painful secrets of victimization is extremely difficult, and in some cases almost impossible, unless the individual has strong emotional resources and there is quality therapeutic intervention as well as family and peer support.

*   *   *

I am vulnerable to meeting the needs of others because I am a twin and because of the lack of effective parenting I received as a child. I know now that I was a victim of emotional and sexual abuse as a child. Like all children who are not properly parented and who are abused, I was not concerned with whether or not I was mistreated. I did what significant other people expected from me to avoid being more abused. This was the way I got through my childhood and adolescence. I was *unable* to think about myself as overly invested in others because I would psychologically and physically risk humiliation or torture if I was concerned for myself. Specifically, I was supposed to look like and behave like my twin sister. I was also expected to take care of her unconditionally. I was supposed to do what my father and brother expected of me. My sense of self-esteem was derived, unfortunately, from people's expectations of me and how I took care of them. I acted out my selflessness as an adolescent and adult in diverse, creative, and oftentimes self-destructive ways. After many years of an effective second psychoanalysis, I have come to understand the extent of the childhood abuse I suffered. I know that I was exploited and victimized so seriously that I repressed the actual details of some of the emotional and sexual abuse. I was a secret survivor. But the secret was uncovered in my second analysis: I was a sex object for my father and brother.

I know now that my relationship with my first analyst was definitely overly selfless and countertherapeutic in terms of self-understanding and self-esteem because the secret of my being sexually abused was never uncovered—it was not even considered. This analysis was productive in terms of outward success and achievement. I was the perfect patient. I did what my first analyst expected of me. Because of my compliance, however, I was victimized by my first analyst as I had been victimized by my family. In the analytic situation I was insidiously seduced into being selfless, into being overly concerned with the needs and judgments of my first analyst. I was always worried about my analyst and his appraisal of me. I spent an enormous amount of time, energy, and money trying to please him. This was just a recreation of my childhood way of interacting. If I was a good child and followed orders, I was spared from abuse. In my first analysis, this meant being a good patient at all times, which meant following my analyst's judgments and prescriptions for my life.

Surely, you are thinking, this is convoluted, outrageous, and horrifying, as I did when I realized what had happened to me. Basically my first analyst did not recognize that I was trying so hard to please him and that my own past way of interacting felt comfortable and safe, since this was the only way I knew how to interact with people. I never questioned whether this was good for me. He never helped me see that I was in a maladaptive pattern that recreated my childhood. Instead of understanding my need to please him as a transference phenomenon, he saw me as the daughter he wanted his own daughter to be. In other words, he chose to ignore this transference issue because my need to please him fulfilled something that he needed for himself. His countertransference was acted out, and I was emotionally exploited.

Hindsight convinces me that my first analyst longed for an achievement-oriented daughter who would obey him and be loyal to his values. Unfortunately for him, his own daughter was quite rebellious and nonconforming. I easily fit into his fantasy need for the high-achieving good daughter. This countertransference was a very serious problem for the analysis in and of itself, but when his daughter became terminally ill, I was unconsciously placed into an unbearable situation, one never openly discussed. Unconsciously, and on a transference level, I fantasized that her death was my fault because I had acted as if I were the good daughter. I feared I had displaced her and destroyed her. An unbearable fantasy, this led me to believe that I needed to help out my analyst in any way possible to stop myself from feeling guilty, from unconsciously believing myself bad and destructive. Of course, this transference reaction, which led me to want to please him in any possible way, should have been "grist for the mill," as they say in analytic circles. My problem with needing to please him at a serious cost to myself should have been understood as a transference issue—that is, an old problem—with roots in my childhood experience. Instead, it became an *enactment*, because Dr. Z liked me to be the good daughter. I did not look at my selfless behavior and my fear of what would happen if I were noncompliant and disappointing to him. Dr. Z didn't seem interested either. He grew dependent on my emotional support.

This transference bondage evolved slowly, but predictably. When Dr. Z's daughter died after five years of suffering from her terminal illness, I unrealistically hated myself for not taking care of Dr. Z properly. I felt inappropriately responsible for a situation that was clearly not my problem. I wanted to die because I felt like such a failure. Dr. Z was suffering, and I could not comfort him. His suffering became my suffering. Set up by Dr. Z's unconscious expectations for me, I became totally over-identified with his pain. Ironically, my own identification with Dr. Z's pain and his need to be cared for allowed me to get in touch with a long, repressed, and serious depression, which had been a mystery to me and Dr. Z. The depression, however, was really no mystery. It grew out of my inability to put my own feelings ahead of others, which was based on my own sense of worthlessness and defectiveness.

* * *

I will back up briefly. I met Dr. Z when I was in my mid-twenties. I was recently married and I had a young baby. My husband was in medical school. I was having reccurring horrible nightmares. In these nightmares, "people come into my bedroom trying to kill me. I wake up in the middle of the night in a panic, sweating and shaking with fear that I had just escaped death."

My husband would calm me down. In addition to my nightmares, I was depressed and felt lost professionally. I hated feeling like I was just a doctor's wife. I knew that I did not want to be a teacher, as my father expected. I had unresolved issues concerning my twinship. I missed my sister, as we had never been separated before we were married within a week of each other. She had left me behind to go to Sweden for one year with her husband. I felt as if I needed to have a close relationship. I wanted to feel whole again. My sister had helped me feel that my life was meaningful. With her absence, I was feeling very lost. I began psychotherapy to get help for myself with these issues of separation and adult identity. However, my effectiveness was sabotaged by Dr. Z, my first analyst. I certainly never intended to become a victim of analysis. I simply wanted help with my intense pain, my overwhelming sense of emptiness, my fears, and the reccurring and terrifying nightmares.

The story grows worse when you look at who and where I was at that time in my life. As well as being a twin, daughter, mother, teacher, graduate student, and doctor's wife, I was the wife of a prospective psychoanalyst. What this translates into in real day-to-day life experience is that I spent a great deal of my free time socializing with other mental health colleagues. I think this left me sheltered from the vulgarities of daily life that one encounters in social situations because helping professionals are by nature concerned people. Usually self-controlled in public, they do not purposely get drunk and then act obnoxious, as ordinary people may do. They do not make passes at you in front of their wives. They talk with you about you. I felt sheltered and cared for by our friends.

I attended countless social functions where friends and colleagues were directly interested in my analysis. My analytic experiences were something I talked about proudly. Being an analysand was a status symbol. I felt proud, for everybody knew that I had a good analyst and that I was doing well. My resume was getting heavier as the years passed. I was writing and having books published, I was teaching, and I was accepting diplomas and certificates. In my social world of mental health professionals, everything seemed more than just okay.

Had I been the wife of a lawyer or even a "regular" medical doctor, more direct, spontaneous questions might have been asked about the purpose of therapy. Most people talk about the cost of therapy and the benefits. They are critical of the process in a genuine way. Are you too close to this person? Is your husband jealous? How long will it take? Is it worth the expense? Most people cannot afford analysis in the first place. So had I married a professor or an artist, I would probably not have had the luxury of psychoanalysis. Had I been single, who knows if I would have become so involved with another man who would not have been a real life-mate.

Here I was, a prospective analyst's wife. I was encouraged to follow the belief that psychoanalysis, at its best, *cures*, and at its worst, helps. I think that my social situation added a factor of unreality that did not prompt me to question or in any way evaluate what was going on in the relationship I had established with my analyst.

You are probably wondering why my husband did not sense that there was something wrong with my analysis. Well, he just kept paying the bills. He never questioned the process until I brought it up. At first his lack of insight was a subject of great debate between us. Now I realize that it was too serious a problem for even my sensitive and insightful husband to figure out. I didn't have any clues myself. Ostensibly, everything was going well. Our children were doing well enough. My life seemed busy and very productive. I wasn't suffering from loneliness or missing my sister. I was extremely high functioning and productive. It was only after many years and intense pain that I got up enough courage to tell my husband my secret—that I could not talk to Dr. Z about his daughter's death. My husband immediately encouraged me to see another analyst to talk about what was happening in my interaction with Dr. Z.

For too many years I blamed myself for the whole catastrophe. Perhaps the truth is that the handwriting was on the wall and I could not see it because I did not know how to read the text in which it was written. So I chose to ignore the clues, which were Dr. Z's judgmentality and rigidity. I often felt that I should have known better. That was when I was being critical of myself. This criticalness is related to the development of an inappropriate sense of responsibility that was encouraged and enforced by my parents. As a child I was supposed to take care of everyone, my father, brother, sister, and mother. So why would I change this pattern and not take care of Dr. Z?

But when I really stop to think about the whole catastrophe, it makes sense. I had never really been cared for consistently by another person. I was brought up to take care of other people. Wanting something for myself was being selfish at best and possibly dangerous. What I ended up doing in my first analysis

was taking care of my analyst—horrifying as it sounds, horrifying as it was. However, given my emotional past, this felt
psychologically safe and easy to do. My reaction really makes
sense in terms of my personality development. But still, it is
really scary and horrifying for me to think that even when individuals in psychotherapy or psychoanalysis want insight into
themselves, they might not get the help and understanding they
need. I know that I am not the first or the last person who will
be victimized by this type of experience. I know that sexually
abused children can easily become analytic victims (Perlman,
1992).

*   *   *

I knew Dr. Z for many years. I knew him as a member of the
psychiatric and psychoanalytic community. He was even my
husband's supervisor in his child psychiatry program for two
years. I knew his wife and family because his children, although
older, went to the same school as my children. Actually, he
recommended that our children go to the same private school
that his children attended. Indirectly, that is how I found out
that Dr. Z's daughter was dying of a rare disease. One night
my husband came home from a hospital staff meeting to tell me
that Dr. Z's daughter, Lonnie, had a rare and deadly disease.
My children knew about her illness because they had heard
about it at school. This was the beginning of the end of Lonnie's
life. It was also the beginning of a serious depression for me.

I remember asking Dr. Z about how ill his daughter really
was. I remember Dr. Z telling me that Lonnie was very ill. He
told me that her illness was very serious and that she might not
live. I felt totally overwhelmed. I wanted to help him. I felt it
was my responsibility to help him. Indeed, I asked him how I
could help. This should have been a red flag of serious concern
for Dr. Z. Instead, he told me that helping him was not a part
of our work together. My need to help him was my *personal*
problem, a symptom of my emotional problems. Dr. Z then

implied that my feelings about his feelings were not a part of our work together. As a therapist I now know that this statement was a sign of his own serious limitations and negligence. For the work of analysis is to understand the interaction between patient and therapist. In hindsight, I see that he was concerned only with protecting his feelings and judgments through the use of his own denial. Afraid of his own feelings, he was also afraid of my feelings.

Verbally and nonverbally, Dr. Z indicated that my feelings of sadness were too much for him to contend with. Knowing this made me feel overwhelmed, trapped with a secret. I felt that I had no one to talk to about our secret, and this feeling unconsciously recreated the same conflict that I had as a child. I was all alone. Dr. Z told me very directly, clearly and emphatically that he did not want to hear about my feelings concerning his daughter's illness. He intimidated me, perhaps unknowingly, by implying that only his really disturbed, borderline (i.e., crazy, incurable) patients were having really strong reactions to his daughter's illness. "Strong reactions," he told me, "were sick." If I could listen to his directions about how to feel about his daughter's illness, then I would be on the road to mental health. I felt confused, devastated, and alone with this prescription for mental health and adaptive functioning. I could not imagine a more horrible loss than the loss of a child. I could not imagine not talking about this with anybody, of keeping this secret. But I did do that to some extent. My husband was in shock over the loss of Dr. Z's daughter. This was an unusually horrible situation. My husband had a difficult time addressing my feelings of despair because he felt overwhelmed himself and, being well-trained as an analyst, did not want to intercede in my relationship with Dr. Z by bringing in his feelings. My friends, those who were not psychiatric colleagues, began to believe that my analysis was really "crazy," and they could not even understand my experiences. So when we were alone driving to school one day, I talked with my eight-year-old daughter, who was very close to me. Intuitively, she could not understand how I was going to keep my sadness to myself. Even at this young age she knew better. "How could you not have feelings about this?" she asked, adding that she thought that Dr. Z was really wrong. She told me that she thought I would need to talk with someone about Dr. Z's daughter's illness. I will always remember this conversation with my daughter and her insight and capacity to understand my despair and her own disdain for secrecy.

But being the good, compliant, caring, and exploitable patient, I did not talk with Dr. Z about his daughter and my feelings about her imminent death. Dr. Z made it very clear that he would discuss neither my feelings nor his about his daughter's illness. I did ask him to tell me about any serious turn of events that might be disturbing to hear about second-hand from my husband or children. He complied with this request by telling me when Lonnie's condition got worse or better. However, he continued to insist indirectly that too much discussion about Lonnie would just indicate that I was an incurable "borderline." He was, in fact, writing a paper on his reactions to his patients who were too disturbed to deal with his daughter's terminal illness. The paper included his estimation of the healthy or objective reaction of patients to a therapist's tragedy. I did not want to be a part of that paper on his personal or countertransference reactions to his crazy patients, so I was compliant to his philosophy of tragedy—to keep it a secret. I had been afraid to speak up as a child because of a realistic fear that I would be abused or tortured. I was afraid to speak up to Dr. Z because of the same fear of being emotionally abused and humiliated. I further trapped myself by believing that my husband might divorce me if I were an incurable borderline patient.

I remember reading Dr. Z's horrible and confusing paper, thinking, "What is he trying to say?" I began to realize that it was he who had problems with his feelings. Compared to Dr. Z, I was the healthy one. But at that point I was unable to listen to my own feelings. I ignored my intuition—those feelings that had gotten me into serious trouble as a child. It was safer to keep them a secret. I acted as if he was right and I was wrong.

Like a good girl, I complied with Dr. Z's mental health program, and for several years Lonnie's death lurked in the back of my mind and in my unconsciousness. I continued to achieve. I finished my two doctorates, graduating at the top of my class. I wrote three books. I got one of the most prestigious training positions in clinical psychology, but I never talked with anybody about my painful feelings, except for that one conversation with my daughter. I was too ashamed, embarrassed that my feelings were bad. I had to hide them, keep them a secret. However, the more I hid my feelings, the more isolated and depressed I got. My accomplishments were important to Dr. Z; meanwhile, to me my life was meaningless. I talked with friends about how difficult it was for Dr. and Mrs. Z and what a tragedy they were confronting. Many of my husband's friends, whom I knew socially, discussed Dr. Z's tragedy with me. What a joke! No one, as I remember, asked me how it was for me. I was too depressed to bring it up myself. I was also too ashamed, and I certainly did not expect anyone to listen to me.

During the last three years of my first analysis, as Lonnie fought a valiant but unsuccessful battle with death, I got more depressed than I ever remember being in my life.

* * *

Depression is something you can identify more clearly after you are no longer depressed. While I was in the middle of this severe depression, I could not see anything in proper perspective. I felt that there was no way out of my pain. I became more and more withdrawn. I felt awful about myself, no matter how well I was doing. By all superficial indications, my analysis was still progressing well because I was achieving. But my analysis really wasn't going well. I spent a lot of time feeling that I could prolong Lonnie's life and minimize Dr. Z's tragedy, especially if I could keep my feelings a secret. When I actually became conscious of my wish to help Lonnie, at the end of her life, I was able to talk about this wish with Dr. Z, who was really horrified on some level. He looked really shocked when I talked about my feelings and my wishes to save him from his pain. But instead of openly admitting to his feelings of concern about our work together, he gave me an interpretation. I will never forget this awful interpretation, which brilliantly got him off the hook. He said that I had tried to take care of him and cure his depression, and that this was what I had tried to do with my mother. His interpretation was absolutely incorrect. My mother was too selfless to allow me to take care of her. This interpretation was his countertransference rationalization. My own realistically encouraged self-sacrificing behavior was my fault again, not his. He refused to take any responsibility for using me as his emotional surrogate daughter. He refused to acknowledge that I had taken care of him by not talking about my pain until it overwhelmed me to the point where I wanted to die. He refused to accept that there were serious problems between us that he had not addressed. A more appropriate comment would have been to acknowledge that he had abused me, just as my father and brother had.

I felt betrayed. This misinterpretation about wanting to cure his depression as a way of curing my mother's depression was a turning point for me. *I knew he was wrong* about what was going on between us and how he interpreted my past. He was covering up his own mistakes! Finally I began to talk to my husband about my secret feelings of despair and my overwhelming depression. I talked about my emotional pain more openly, in spite of my shame and fear of not being listened to as well as my fear of getting into trouble. As I spoke up, my dear friends and colleagues began to listen to my story about Dr. Z. In a heart-to-heart talk, my best friend in my training program in clinical psychology told me that I was in fact underreacting to the tragedy. She most emphatically suggested that I get an outside consultation. She was seriously concerned about me.

When Lonnie died, Dr. Z called and invited me to the funeral, and then he called back to tell me that the funeral was limited to the immediate family. I was so offended and hurt. I felt used by this crazy-making situation with him. For several months I cancelled all of my appointments. In desperation and with the help of my family and dear friends and colleagues, I consulted another analyst. The consensus of my husband, friends, and an outside consultant was that I was overidentified with Dr. Z or felt too responsible for his problem. But then I also felt responsible and ashamed that I was overidentified with Dr. Z. My shame and humiliation was painful and debilitating.

I feel now that I was exploited by Dr. Z, who used my concern to deal with the loss of his daughter instead of his own feelings. I believe my feelings and suffering for him protected him from his own heart-wrenching loss. I can even understand his need for me, and my concerns for him; but I know that he was nonetheless inappropriate because he burdened me with his unconscious expectation that I help him suffer. In other words, I suffered for him, as I suffered for others in my childhood. As I write these words, I understand what happened even more clearly. I had been mentally abused. I had been victimized. My selflessness had hurt me. I was drowning in my own depression. I was lost. I felt that I was no longer entitled to my psychological needs when Lonnie died. I felt that I was not worthy of my life, as if I had done something wrong. Everything was black. Everything was meaningless. I had no right to express these feelings. I thought, "No one, even my own family, must know my sense of despair." I believe now, in looking back, that my feeling states related to being sexually abused were beginning to surface. Being emotionally exploited once again made me feel bad, guilty, ashamed about myself, as I had felt when I was exploited as a child. Like other sexually abused children, I learned that no matter what happens, it is my fault. That was my reaction, plain and simple. I felt ashamed and guilty for being abused, just as I had felt as a child.

* * *

At that time I had no awareness of childhood memories, of such deep depression, of such utter despair and hopelessness, because these memories and feelings had been disavowed and then repressed. I had disassociated from them, which is a common phenomenon for survivors of sexual abuse (Blume, 1989; Frederickson, 1992). My memories of abuse had totally disappeared from my awareness.

At that time, I could remember, as a ten-year-old, when my friend's mother died, I felt a sadness and loss that was extremely upsetting. I developed a sense of the meaning of mortality.

I could remember at 21, three days before my wedding, being separated from my twin sister for the first time when she and her new husband went to Europe for one year. I felt an overwhelming loneliness. I felt empty and came to recognize just how much I counted on her to help me make decisions and give direction to my life. I missed her in a profound way. Even then I did not feel this unique sense of despair in which I was now lost—the sense that my life was totally meaningless and not worth living.

Yet I had no sense of what my reaction was related to in my own life because I had no memories to connect to the reaction. I could understand intellectually the theoretical construct of overidentification, which made sense to me. I was a twin, and I knew that twins were vulnerable to getting too close to each other because of their early primal bond with one another. But I could not understand why I wanted to give up living. Why was this even an option that I had a fantasy about? If I sacrificed myself so that Dr. Z's pain would go away, I felt, the problem would be solved. This is what I had done as a child when I was abused. If I allowed my father and brother to abuse me, which was a form of psychological annihilation, then perhaps they would leave me alone for a while. Being psychologically abused and annihilated was a way of getting away from other types of incestuous pain.

I cannot say exactly when or how I learned this way of relating—to sacrifice my existence to make another individual feel better about who he was. I am sure that I was used as a sacrifice very early in my childhood and for a long period of time. I am sure that I was made to sacrifice myself emotionally and sexually to make others feel better about themselves. On some deep level, this is what happened again, what was recreated when I fell back into the regression of self-sacrifice with Dr. Z. Actually, I began to reexperience the abuse I had suffered. In some perverse way, it helped me to look deeper into myself.

I know now that there are easier ways to get back to the pain of sexual abuse. There are easier and more compassionate ways to recover forgotten feelings and memories.

THREE

Breaking through My Despair

Lost in the seriousness of my depression and despair, I was able to trust my own sense that there were serious problems with my first analysis. Years of analysis and a serious personal loss to my analyst had brought to the surface of my awareness long-repressed emotional memories of childhood abuse and depression.

Although Dr. Z never came to accept that there was a problem with my treatment, I decided that I had had enough psychoanalysis with him. We began to terminate the treatment. In doing so we talked about what I had learned about myself and how the analysis had helped my career. Dr. Z and I discussed what might be left unexplored in my psyche. I was finally open with Dr. Z about feeling overwhelmed about what I had experienced during the two-month break we took after his daughter's funeral. Knowing that he too was suffering, I carefully tried to explain how I felt trapped in my life, which seemed even more meaningless now that his daughter was dead.

Initially he seemed truly concerned and puzzled by my reaction. Speaking frankly, I described to him how I had tried to help myself understand why my life now seemed meaningless by consulting a highly reputable analyst recommended by a well-respected friend and colleague of mine. Unimpressed with my decision, he showed no concern for my feelings about the consultant's opinion or for other people's reaction, even my husband's. When I insisted that he listen, he became angry. In fact, he reacted defensively when I told him that the other consulting analyst thought we were overidentified. I know now that my problem was even more serious than overidentification; I had been emotionally exploited. I had been victimized.

Whereas I was impressed with the new insight and able to understand the consulting analyst's opinion, Dr. Z was unimpressed. He felt that I had consulted the wrong professional. The consultant I had chosen was of a different theoretical viewpoint and not a member of the same group of analysts as Dr. Z. I knew that Dr. Z's opinion about which doctor I had consulted for advice was another defensive maneuver. Dr. Z just didn't want to hear what I had to say. He quickly dismissed the issue of my overidentification. Again, his message to me was that *I should stop trying to act out my need to cure my mother's depression*. I should, in his view, be more realistic about my limitations and less emotional "for his sake." He attributed the problem, as he had always done, to my unresolved emotionality and did not, or could not, acknowledge how he had inadvertently recreated my worst childhood emotional traumas. Had he tried to understand the intensity of my changing emotional states, then I wouldn't have been so traumatized by his method of treatment.

But underneath his defensiveness, despite his interpretations, he knew he had hurt me. He just could not admit it. I think that he had regrets about our work. Whether these regrets included my treatment or just sadness that I had been so negatively affected by his loss, I really cannot say. After his daughter's death, he seemed like a fallen man. He seemed so devastated and fragile. I still feel extremely sorry for him in his loss and hope never to suffer a loss of one of my own children.

We tried to terminate the analysis properly, but that proved impossible. He had encouraged me to develop and maintain an idealized sense of our work together. He wanted me to continue to respect his sensibility and accept his judgment without question. *He was really so similar to my father and brother. He had forgotten that interpretation.* Even then I knew that we had not adequately confronted in therapy my own anger at him. His lack of capacity to tolerate my intense feelings had prevented the resolution of my negative feelings of rage. Although he once admitted, "We have not worked through the negative transference," I had not understood how serious this problem was in our work together. Now I understand that this statement about not working through the negative transference was a "red flag" that symbolized my emotional revictimization.

*   *   *

I was very confused about what I had accomplished in my lengthy first analysis. I was clearly a successful professional woman. Although still eager to achieve, I felt unbalanced by my driven behavior and did not feel as successful as I looked to the outside world. I found myself driven to achieve to feel good about myself—for the moment. As hard as I tried, I could not hold on to a good sense of myself. I did not know what to do about my poor self-esteem. I felt lost in a bottomless pit. I was miserable when I thought that I was not doing everything perfectly, even though I knew being perfect all the time was impossible. It was stupid to try so hard. Yet I could not emotionally accept my own limitations, even though I knew in my head that I should. I knew that I was not taking care of myself. I knew that I was just covering up a very serious problem.

My husband and children were aware that I was seriously depressed, but understandably, they could not grasp what was wrong with me. My daughter said, "Some people read three books a year. You write them, Mommy. I don't know why you have to work so hard." She was right. I was driving myself extremely hard, yet I also got discouraged very easily. I was not myself. I was harder on myself and felt more pressured than was normal, even for me. I knew that I had gotten *worse* in analysis with Dr. Z.

I labeled my new state of mind an existential depression. What that meant to me was that I felt intensely that my life was totally meaningless. This feeling persisted on and off for a year and a half. I believe on reflection that those feeling states were a mirror of the original childhood traumatic states I had experienced. At my worst point the depression was totally consuming and terrifying. I was afraid to drive past the cemetery where Lonnie was buried, for example, because I would immediately feel devastated and confused about the meaning of my life. I tried to talk with my husband about my despair, but he did not really understand. Confused about what I called my existential crisis, he grew tired hearing me talk about the meaninglessness of life. From his vantage point, my life was extremely busy and productive. Of course I now know that what I was really talking about was my emotional memories of childhood sexual abuse, not the meaninglessness of my life. But at that time nobody could unravel the secret code under the depression.

My husband is a fine, kind, and devoted person, a well-trained psychiatrist-psychoanalyst, and a practical man. In an attempt to get me out of my misery, he would say to me, "You know you have to take that freeway to go to the airport, so if you have to get so extremely upset every time we drive by the cemetery, we will not go anywhere." He thought his threat would work because I am an enthusiastic and energetic traveler and a highly persistent individual. He thought I could and should be able to get on the freeway and just get out of town, but I could not. I was totally overwhelmed—I felt like a horrendous failure. I had finally reached my feelings and memories about my childhood but was unable to identify them as such. My existential crisis persisted. I simply could not get over the sense that my life was meaningless. I could not decode the pain.

Rightly so, my husband grew impatient. He tired of my continuing obsessiveness about the meaninglessness of my life and of my withdrawal. In desperation, and half in jest, he even told me one day that he would prescribe antidepressant medication if I could not decide which new convertible I wanted him to buy for me. Did I want a BMW or a Saab convertible? My husband was totally puzzled and concerned. Why couldn't I decide? He was also extremely lonely, and I remained extremely sad. Trying to help me, he talked about more treatment—another analysis. This idea of starting over, of talking with someone else about my life, at first just went in one ear and out the other, although I did think about what options I had in terms of analysts I knew through our personal and professional contacts.

The unexpected news of my father's terminal cancer was what made me realize that I needed to understand my depression. A trip to Europe, a new convertible, and helping my own patients understand and resolve their own depressions were not enough to help me think that my life was worthwhile. Publishing a new book did not solve the problem of making my depression go away, either.

I am not sure what triggered me to speak up, but one night, without knowing exactly what started my sadness and despair—most likely I had had a discouraging conversation with my twin sister—I said to my husband, "I need more help." My husband, whose motto is "strike while the iron is hot," immediately seized the moment and called one of his most respected colleagues at home. He explained briefly how very depressed I was about Dr. Z and my analysis with him, and he asked his respected colleague to call me the next day.

I remember that first phone call with my new analyst vividly. I talked to him from my own office. I said that I was depressed about my treatment with Dr. Z and was unable to psychologically integrate the death of Dr. Z's daughter. I related the consultant's diagnosis of overidentification. The new analyst, Dr. Ace, listened as I explained that sometimes my self-esteem was very weak and in those moments I would lose any good feelings about myself. My depression concerned him. He talked with me on the phone for 20 minutes about my feelings. He also listened very carefully.

I thought, while talking to him, "This doctor is not using that 'big' word, overidentification." He did not need to put a label on my experience in my previous analysis or to neatly categorize it. Dr. Ace understood that my experiences and changing states of mind were completely overwhelming to me. He did not sound angry or judgmental about the fact that I had gotten myself into this mess. He did not sound busy or preoccupied. I knew he had a waiting list for new patients, but this didn't come up in our conversation. So I made an appointment to see him the next day. Only after hanging up the telephone did I realize how terrified I was to meet him. I was glad he was not difficult to talk to on the telephone. In fact, I had liked talking with him.

At our first meeting I found Dr. Ace to be a rather serious man. Later, in that first week of treatment, I was much relieved to find out that he had gone through analysis twice himself. He was very kind, very patient, and most concerned about my problem, which he said was quite *unfortunate*. His demeanor was calm, nonthreatening. But I was still terrified of saying anything that might be judged foolish or silly. The domineering nature of Dr. Z still permeated my conscious and unconscious thoughts. How would I explain to him who I was? What had happened to me? And where should I begin? I had gone over the fact that I was a twin millions of times. I had even written my dissertation and a book on the subject of twin development. I ruled out the twin issue as a core problem for myself (Schave, 1982; Schave & Ciriello, 1983). I was right!

For my first appointment I brought my resume for Dr. Ace to see. This gesture certainly made an impression. Dr. Ace was really different than Dr. Z, who had helped me compile my resume and who had kept tabs on what I was doing. He looked totally shocked when I handed him my resume. He walked slowly over to his desk with my resume in his hand and put it down. I imagined what he was thinking as he walked to his desk, "What is this nonsense of giving me your resume? What is it supposed to mean?" I immediately felt compelled by this little man, who seemed very careful about what he had to say to me. He knew I was overwhelmed and depressed, that my life was out of balance. I sensed that he was trying to understand my feelings without being the expert. He thought I should be the expert on my feelings.

Dr. Ace was not mean about my resume, nor was he callous. He could have said, "This is not a job interview or an audition," but he didn't say anything. In his own understated and non-judgmental way, he conveyed his sense that I was overly invested in my achievements and not invested enough in myself. He was exactly right, of course, but it was difficult to hear what he had to say or to think about his observations, as the truth can be powerfully painful. I knew that I needed to understand why my resume had gotten so much attention from Dr. Z, while my good feelings about myself had been so seriously neglected.

I agreed to see Dr. Ace on a regular basis. Initially I felt as if I was in supervision for myself about myself. It was as if Dr. Schave were going to talk to Dr. Ace about Dr. Schave. This was really true. I dispassionately explained the psychodynamics Dr. Z and I had worked on long and hard to understand. Born and raised in a Jewish neighborhood in Los Angeles, I have a large extended Jewish family. My uncle was the rabbi of our congregation. All my aunts, uncles, and cousins are upwardly mobile professionals and artists. I have a twin sister. Based on his introspection, Dr. Z had decided that I was the bad twin, but the competent one of the pair. I have an older, sadistic brother who is a genius. My father was passive and very critical of everything and everyone. My mother was very bright, depressed, and dominated by my father and brother. I was the one who took care of everyone's needs in my family. This included always being second best to my twin sister, who was always the good one, always right, no matter what trouble she was causing. In short, I came from a high-achieving extended family who on the outside looked as if they had it all. Underneath the facade, however, were emotional problems and corruption.

*   *   *

I was not going to overidentify with my new analyst. At first
I was terrified to see him outside the walls of his office, at a
party, for example, or to ask him about his family. But in spite
of my conscious and unconscious resistances to connecting to
him emotionally, I did. I remember feeling it was too difficult
to talk about my experiences with Dr. Ace only once weekly. I
needed more contact with him, but I was not going to get too
involved. In spite of my conscious attempt to keep my distance,
my first dream about Dr. Ace was that he died and his wife
called to tell me. I was horrified but at the same time relieved
that I was emotionally connecting with him. It terrified me. I
had vowed not to let this happen again, for I did not want to
be dependent on anyone ever again. Thinking back, I am extremely thankful that Dr. Ace wanted to connect with my feelings, and that I perceived that Dr. Ace believed my feelings were
important. This was my first step on the road to recovery.

As I now think about what happened in the initial phase of
work with my new analyst, Dr. Ace, I see that we were on the
right track. I found myself slowly listening to my own feelings
and using these feelings to make decisions on my own behalf.
My thoughts and theories about the best way to function slowly
became secondary to my feelings. I remember saying to myself
that I felt as if I needed more time with Dr. Ace. To my surprise,
I did not feel critical of myself or overemotional, nor did I feel
an immediate need to understand why. I just made more appointments to see him.

Actually, Dr. Ace really was taken aback. He was shocked by
Dr. Z's notion that I was overemotional. (I think that Dr. Ace
likes my passionate sensibility and thinks that the notion that
one can be overemotional is absurd in the analytic situation.)
He cleverly suggested that I had been involved in career counseling, not in psychoanalysis. I knew he was right, but emotionally it took me years to accept the ramifications of this simple
idea.

* * *

I do not want you to think that I just drove over to Dr. Ace's office in my new convertible with my fear in my pocket and that I emptied out my fears in one session, like dumping one pail of sand onto the cement. It was more like I had a large sandy beach of fearfulness to empty out of my heart. Then, I didn't know if I was acting courageously or very foolishly, but I decided to try again. Actually, I never thought about a second analysis in this way. I never said to myself, "Why try this again? It did not work the first time." I tried to stay away from thinking that my first analysis had failed me. But I knew my fearfulness was there, lurking just below consciousness.

I dealt with the idea of a second analytic experience from that part of myself that was invested in the process of psychoanalysis as a valuable part of my life. I believed in my professional identity as a clinical psychologist. I could tell from my own experiences as a therapist that I helped people to understand themselves and to feel better about their life choices, as well as their past and present experiences. I wanted for myself what I was able to give to others.

Dr. Ace knew that I was smart enough to intellectualize the need for a second analytic experience, but he was also smart enough to know that I was not coming in to see him because he was a training analyst and I was considering joining his psychoanalytic institute. He knew that I was in emotional trouble because of the combination of my intellectual capacity, my sensitivity, and my need to put other people's feelings first.

Although he admitted later in our work that he thought I had what it took to be an analyst (this was not necessarily stated as a compliment), this was not his main concern—to recruit me for his analytic institute. His first concern was my feelings about our initial contact. Why didn't I call him? Why did I let my husband do this for me? Who was making this decision to seek therapy? Was I sure that he was the right analyst? I had needed

my husband's help to call him, I assured Dr. Ace. But I had
chosen him carefully, and that choice was mine alone.

I think that Dr. Ace's line of critical questioning was a smart
move on his part. He made me take responsibility for my feelings
about what had happened to me. He did not try to diffuse or,
worse, to avoid my feelings, as Dr. Z had done. He talked with
me about how hard it must be for me to see another analyst
after such an extremely painful experience in analysis with Dr.
Z. We both knew, though it was never stated, that I would need
a long time to develop trust before I could even start to deal
with the profound and intense hurt that had brought me back
into analysis. What helped me to trust Dr. Ace was his ability
to acknowledge the pain I had experienced both as a child and
as a patient. He offered hope without being arrogant or self-
righteous. He balanced his statements about Dr. Z so that I did
not experience him as needing to be better than Dr. Z. He just
understood that I was confused about my life circumstances and
my fluctuating states of mind and self-esteem.

I, of course, was thinking about the problems—in supervision
for myself about myself. I discussed the problems Dr. Z had
ignored. Besides being depressed and wanting to sacrifice my
life for others, I knew that I had avoided two big issues in my
sessions with Dr. Z. First, I told Dr. Ace that I had never talked
with Dr. Z about sex. Dr. Z had told me that he believed I was
comfortable with my sexuality and *that was why I didn't want to
talk about it*. This was clearly a false assumption because I knew
that when some patients talked with me about their sexual experiences, I became very anxious and oftentimes sick to my
stomach. I told Dr. Ace that my husband thought I had difficulty
with erotic countertransferences with my patients. In other
words, patients' stories of their sexual experiences were difficult
for me to listen to—they were overstimulating to me. Second,
I explained to Dr. Ace that it was impossible for Dr. Z to accept
that I was angry with him, which made me both sad and horrified. I felt that I had not worked through the negative transference and that I was confused by my first analysis. "Sexuality

and negative transferences were the clinical issues that needed to be addressed" was my clinical pronouncement and assessment. I was busy writing a psychological evaluation of myself to keep my distance from my distress, holding on to my psychobabble labels to keep myself from feeling the pain.

During the first six months of my work with Dr. Ace, I felt I was one step removed from my problems. I was removed from the person I was talking about. I felt really strange, but I believe it was an understandable reaction against getting hurt again. As I think back on the beginning sessions, I recognize that I was talking about a part of myself that I had never before been able to get out, *my feelings*. Fortunately, I was able to bond with Dr. Ace because he made me feel that my feelings were what mattered more than my thoughts. He believed, even though the details were still a mystery, that I could understand what had gone wrong in my first analysis and what had happened to me as a child to allow me to recreate a self-sacrificing relationship in which I was emotionally victimized. His continual hopefulness that I could come to understand myself better gradually allowed me to regain faith in the integrity of my feelings and what I wanted for myself. I regained a belief that I could profit from analysis. I was getting less depressed.

*   *   *

Dr. Ace's hopefulness was crucial in my eventual recovery of memories and self-understanding. My insights about what had happened to me as a child were based on Dr. Ace's ability to stay connected with my feelings, instead of focusing on my ideas and theories. Getting in touch and concentrating on my feelings was a difficult task that took enormous persistence. Dr. Ace still reminds me how difficult it was for me to identify my feelings when we first started our work together. He admits that he needed to be extremely persistent with me in order to get me to concentrate on my feelings, instead of my ideas and theories.

It was my feelings that led me to understand the truths about my childhood.

FOUR

Confrontations with the Past

Confrontation as an emotional experience is highly subjective, personal, and almost solitary. Ironically, this type of naked vulnerability can easily be misunderstood by both the patient and the analyst. Perhaps this is true because emotional confrontation is a complicated "underground" experience, as compared to a military confrontation, where the intent and devastation are obvious. For example, the reason for the bombing of Hiroshima and the devastation left behind is easily apparent to any observer and to both sides. But emotional confrontation—that is, a direct challenge of an experience or interaction—is not as observable to the naked eye. It is not necessarily a singular, concrete experience that can be documented in black and white. There is probably no consensus about the intentions of an emotional confrontation or about the amount of destruction it causes. Divorce is an example. It is an emotional confrontation that is devastating to an individual, but often the feelings associated with divorce are elusive and diffuse to the observer. There is usually no agreement as to the measurable amount of damage.

Nevertheless, given the misunderstandings that are possible, I will still use the concept of emotional confrontation in relationship to my feelings about my first analytic experience. Trusting my feelings that I must confront my first analyst allowed me to arrive at a new understanding about my childhood. I am sure that Dr. Z would tell his side of the story differently. He might say that I was unanalyzable and untreatable by his analytic method. Actually, sexually abused women commonly hear this excuse when the deep issues of their traumatic experiences are not uncovered by psychotherapeutic treatment. Recent research indicates that survivors of sexual abuse often have many therapeutic encounters before they get in touch with what really caused their self-hatred (Courtois, 1988; Perlman, 1992). Perlman (in press) states;

> I have worked with many incest and child abuse survivors who have been treated for years for physical disorders. Upon analytic treatment, these disorders often turn out to be, in the patient's view and mine, the body memories of physical and sexual abuse.
> . . .
> These patients have had psychotherapy before, some with as many as six or seven therapists. Often lacking in these treatments was two fundamental elements: (1) the ability of the therapist to sit with the patient through the reporting and reliving of extremely painful material, without denying his or her experience; and (2) the ability of the therapist to engender a pre-Oedipal transference. The patient must have a deep, close experience of the analyst as a good object; but beyond this, the patient may need a merger with the "powerful analyst/mother." . . .
> When this powerful material is mishandled, the development of a pre-Oedipal transference is blocked, which usually aborts any meaningful treatment for incest survivors. (pp. 7–8)

*   *   *

Tragically, when I began to talk with Dr. Ace about the disappointment and unfinished business from my first analysis, I became aware that I could not bring back visual or emotional memories about my life inside the walls of my parent's house. When I closed my eyes to remember, there was only darkness. *I remembered nothing that happened within the interior of the house.*

This is still a horrifying truth for me. I can very clearly remember exterior memories, however: the school yard and Girl Scouts and going to synagogue. I had to face the reality that I had amnesia about most of my childhood experiences and that I had not talked about this with Dr. Z or, worse yet, thought about it.

I retained but two memories from inside my parents' house, memories that were vivid and powerful throughout my life. First, I remember that at around the age of six I walked out of my bedroom screaming at my family to turn down the television because I couldn't sleep with all the noise. Dr. Z never explored this memory. Why was I so afraid of noise? What happened when it was too noisy? This memory was a clue to my past that still remained unexplored.

I also remember once playing hot foot, or footsie, in my parents' living room with my older brother and twin sister. My sister remembers that we played this game a lot. I can only remember playing it once! This was a game we played when my parents went out of town. My sister and I were eight or nine. My brother was 16. My brother would stick matches between my toes while my sister sat next to me. She would just watch what my brother was doing. He would then light the matches to see if I would blow them out or if I would just let myself get burned. The challenge for me in this game was twofold. Primarily I was not to get burned, but I was also extremely careful not to be called a chicken by my brother and sister. The trick was not to blow out the matches too soon. In other words, winning meant pushing myself to the edge of destruction without falling apart completely. This was a complicated way of interacting, to say the least.

The game of footsie was the basis of my character structure. I think that this pattern of letting myself be abused and tortured yet accepting it as okay became a way of interacting with the world. This type of self-destructiveness is common in individuals who have been abused. Victims of abuse have a limited sense of the seriousness of their vulnerability. They have inadequate personality resources to deal with self-protection and thus use the denial of pain as a way of coping. I, like most if not all victims of abuse, saw pain and humiliation as a way of life.

I remember that I always won our game of hot foot. I also remember thay my mother knew that we played this game. She seemed ashamed that my brother was the ring leader of this cruel game. However, she couldn't stop us from playing the game. As a young adult, I confronted my brother with his role as a bully in our game of hot foot. He was not at all remorseful, but he was afraid that someone might find out about it. He asked me not to talk to his girlfriend about this particular "fun" situation that he had set up for us to play. The important thing for him was that we keep the game a secret among ourselves. He didn't apologize for his sadistic behavior. Indeed, he still thinks that our game was cute.

Recently my sister and I spoke about her passive role in the game of footsie. In November 1992 she shared her feelings with me.

> I sat next to you and did nothing because it was my role in the family. I was a child and I didn't know that it was more than a game. And I was led to believe that allegiances to Alan were crucial because he had all the power in the family. I am sorry that I didn't know better. I feel furious and frustrated that he un- knowingly made me hurt you and myself and that as an adult he won't accept responsibility for what he did. I feel like we are still trapped in this story, because he can't accept what he did.

*   *   *

I had only these two intact memories available to my conscious mind when I began my first psychoanalysis with Dr. Z. He was totally shocked and horrified by the sadistic game. Dr. Z became my ally in hating my brother. My memory of this game became the basis of his, and then our, understanding of my life expe- riences. I was the bad self-sacrificing twin, my sister was the good but unreliable twin sister. My brother was the bully, the torturer. My parents were participants in keeping this triangle alive. My father and brother believed that I was bad and that my sister was good. Afraid to challenge my father and brother, my mother was a tortured victim of their abuse as well. She was afraid to speak up for fear of further victimization. She was trapped in her own poor self-esteem, which did not allow her to believe she could survive on her own without my father and brother. I don't think that she ever believed that I was bad. She tried to give me a sense of freedom, and she did. She accepted my unique qualities, but she couldn't protect me from my tyrannical father and brother because of her own victimization as a child. My strength as an individual came from my mother's affection and attention.

Dr. Z's intellectualized hypothesis about the split in my twinship was the work or the understanding that I integrated in my first analysis. Dr. Z's hypothesis about the good and bad twin made a lot of sense to me while I was in analysis with Dr. Z. I felt that he understood my experience of being a twin as well as he could, not being a twin himself. It was reassuring to feel understood. I got over feeling like a freak. In fact, I did research with other twins and found out that labeling twins as good and bad is a common, yet pathological twin bonding experience (Schave & Ciriello, 1983). At first I was relieved and reassured to know that other twins had been parented in the same way that my sister and I had been parented.

Looking back, I now believe that Dr. Z's hypothesis that I was bad and my sister good was nearly lethal to both of us. It was in many ways more cruel than the sexual abuse I suffered as a child because it was a view given from a professional in a position of authority as a form of medical treatment. Although my incestuous experiences were certainly malignant, they were not a medical service that I had sought out and paid for. Incest was something that happened within the chaos of my family's structure. In comparison, Dr. Z's hypothesis that I was bad and Marjorie was good was given as a truthful interpretation of reality from a position of power and knowledge. As a result of this hypothesis, my sister and I became totally estranged. A rift widened between us, creating an emotional abyss, an empty hole that was painful to face. The abyss created a self-imposed spiritual death sentence for both of us. It was as if Dr. Z had cut out part of our soul. I was, of course, emotionally blinded by the loss of my sister, and she in turn suffered from our estrangement in her own painful and profound way.

In reality, my sister and I have a very complicated relationship that now affords us a great deal of emotional comfort and creative stimulation. We are very different people, but there are no labels that can define who we are as individuals and who we are as twins. We appreciate and enjoy our differences as well as our closeness.

So my baseline knowledge of family dynamics had something missing and was totally distorted. The real truth was that I felt inherently defective. I didn't understand why I had to push myself so hard. I didn't understand why I had so much invested, metaphorically speaking, in playing with fire and not getting burned. I didn't understand my need to recreate being a victim. There were secrets in my past that remained unexplored, secrets that I couldn't know about or understand because I had amnesia.

Dr. Ace immediately got into my memories of the game of footsie. He asked me to think about my feelings about playing the game. Was I aware that I was the victim? Did I wonder why? Relating the game of footsie to my feelings began to create a breakthrough to understanding my past.

*   *   *

My ability to focus on the past was interrupted when my father was dying of cancer. My mother was hospitalized for a severe depression after caring for him alone, full time, for far too many years. My sister, brother, and I had to work together once again. The triangle was reestablished because the relationships were the same, even though we were older and totally self-sufficient.

My brother was still the "busy genius," the bully, the Mr. Know-it-all. My sister was still the chosen judge, watching to see how much abuse I could take before she protected me. I was again set up to be burned if I played with both of them. So I didn't talk with them because I knew better this time. Still, this was a terrifying time of my life. Being with my brother and sister before my father died was an unbearable situation. I felt that being with my sister and brother was equivalent to walking into a Nazi concentration camp. My sister might just let go of my hand. I might be thrown into the gas chamber at any time. I can vividly remember nightmares with the same theme, where *I am abandoned by my sister and then tortured by my brother*. These nightmares were frequent in the beginning of my second analysis.

I can only imagine that as a child I was always verbally abused by my father and brother, and as an adult the pattern continued for them, but not for me. I was no longer their victim. To avoid abuse, I avoided any contact with my father and brother. During the three-month period before my father died, I tried to work with my sister on arrangements. Because my mother had been briefly hospitalized for depression, I became my mother's psychotherapist and social worker in order to nurse her back to sanity. I remember my mother's psychiatrist commenting that I always made 45-minute visits to the hospital, that I acted as if I were on the hospital staff. I think he appreciated my concern and my capacity to be effective. I did help my mother, for she was able to return home and care for my father before he died.

My father's last months of life and his death were an ongoing nightmare that I spoke about to my second analyst. My understanding and experience as the bad but competent twin were enacted by the family as if I were still a child. Knowing the psychodynamics of the family, I tried to stay above water and not drown in the past chaos and humiliation. I tried to hold on to my good feelings about myself. Dr. Ace was able to assist me with this difficult situation because he was careful to take my feelings more seriously than my ideas. Dr. Z had encouraged me only to be in control of my life. In contrast, Dr. Ace encouraged me only to take my feelings seriously, to stay away from my brother and sister, and not to see my father if I feared I would be emotionally abused. Theories about what I should do to demonstrate my strength as an individual were put on the back burner. Dr. Ace was not concerned about how brave I could be. He did not encourage me to get involved in the old game of footsie. He encouraged me to give up my self-sacrificing identity, and I was eager to do so. Consequently, I never saw my father before he died and I have no regrets that I did not say goodbye to him. I knew that we would just fight and I would be hurt. I did not want to suffer from his abuse.

I retain one important memory from the end of my father's life, amidst my vigilance to avoid the pain of his criticism. I remember that my father *called me* on my office phone three days before he died. He told me, "Take care of your mother." He said, "You are a doctor, you will know what to do with her." My father believed that my mother would be unable to function without his abuse and his direction. He feared she would be declared insane when he was gone. His direction, "Take care of your mother," was one of the few times that my father talked to me as if I were a significant human being, someone with some value to him. Or perhaps this was another manipulation. Perhaps he just wanted to be sure that I got hurt again. He had written me out of his will, so I would not forget that I was his bad, defective, worthless child. Perhaps he hoped I might abandon my mother, when I knew what he had done to me, when I knew how much he hated me. But he was wrong. After my father's death, my mother and I became extremely close and open with each other.

As an adult I had always imagined that my father would write me out of his will. But the experience of seeing the will was more horrifying and overwhelming than I had ever imagined, even though I was intellectually prepared for being cut out of the will because I hated my father and he hated me. I knew that it was going to immortalize his disdain for me. But it hurt me deeply when I saw it in black and white. It was too real, too painful. It was traumatic. There was no comfort in knowing the family dynamics. I felt like an outcast. I was shocked and over-whelmed by my father's cruelty.

Dr. Ace helped me through this devastating time of my life. He was extremely kind, patient, and tolerant of my pain. I began to feel closer to him. I felt protected as he helped me accept the reality of my feelings about my father. My concern about why I was the family outcast was not in the forefront of our work. I needed analytic crisis counseling at that point. I needed com-passion and understanding, and this is what I received. Getting the emotional attention I needed was crucial. I was able to rely less on my hard-learned intellectual defenses and theoretical speculations. I had to feel the pain of being bad, instead of thinking that I was the bad child in my family.

In retrospect, I think that Dr. Ace took a militant stance against my theoretical reflections about my place in the family. Some-times I told him that he didn't understand what my need to understand myself intellectually really meant to me. There were times when I don't think he really cared that I was capable of deep intellectual insights. My theories got in the way of my emotional experiences, and Dr. Ace wanted to hear only about my emotional experiences. This adjustment from intellectual speculation to owning my feelings and experiences was difficult yet crucial. Dr. Ace was hard on me, and in turn he had to work hard, when he wanted me to stay with my feelings and my experiences. As hard as it is to do, I feel that getting out of my head and into my own sensibility or feelings is what has made me a more resilient individual and a better therapist and it has led me to remember the secrets of my past.

* * *

The summer after my father died, my husband took me and our children to Europe. I had always dreamed of a European vacation. I think that my husband knew that I needed this type of holiday. It was good for me to get what I had dreamed of and longed for, an experience that was extremely foreign to me. I loved it. I learned that I could be expansive, that I could get what I wanted from life and not hurt other people.

I knew when I returned home from Europe that I was on the way to recovering my own sense of entitlement. The depression began to lessen. I could drive on the freeway and not feel that my life was meaningless, even when I passed the cemetery where Lonnie was buried. I began to consider a more direct approach to my life. Maybe I just needed to take what I wanted from life. I needed to be more practical, just as my husband had originally suggested. I needed to value my life just as much as anyone else's life. Practicality was the way out of my emotional turmoil, which ranged from always feeling less than adequate to hating myself. My husband's practicality saved me, even though I fought with him a lot about his more concrete approach to life.

My second analyst was and still is practical, sincere, understanding, and driven. I think that being driven was what Dr. Z lacked, and this is what limited our work together. I needed to find someone who was as intensely perfectionistic as I was and am, but who also knew how to handle that drive for perfection. When it's working, perfectionism is fine, for it enables you to be proud of your accomplishments. But when perfectionism traps you, by limiting your choices in life, you are open to neurosis, unhappiness, and loneliness. Dr. Z wasn't a perfectionist. He just wanted to do his job the best that he could, and he did just that. He stayed on the surface. But my second analyst was driven to be accurate, and he was always aware of what was happening in our interaction in my analysis. He was never willing to settle for feeling that we understood each other or thinking that he knew what was good for me. Although Dr. Ace was always concerned with my sadness and depression and what had triggered the feelings, he never said, "You'll feel better soon." This was Dr. Z's demeaning approach to my depression, predicting how long I would be unhappy or suggesting what I could do to feel better. Dr. Z wasn't concerned with the roots of my feelings, he was interested only in how I functioned.

Dr. Ace wanted to reflect my state of mind accurately. It was more important for him to be attuned to me than to think that he knew exactly what was going to happen to me in my emotional life. Whereas Dr. Ace rarely gave me advice, Dr. Z always knew what I should do. Dr. Ace showed me he believed in me by making me an equal partner in my analysis. I had to take responsibility for my success and happiness as well as for my sense of despair. I had to figure out how to solve my own problems and how to take them more seriously than other people's problems.

When I returned from the Swiss alps, Dr. Ace was ready for our analytic adventure. He had figured out that I was a totally driven human being—driven to do things right. So he said to me, "Why don't we do this right?" I was totally perplexed. I looked at him as if he were crazy because he knew that I didn't want to fail in my second analysis. Once in a blue moon Dr. Ace took time out from his experiential, subjective approach to psychoanalysis to lecture to me on his theory that analysis and graduate school were opposite experiences. "Graduate school is based on achievement, analysis is based on feelings," he lectured. I thought that I wasn't getting grades from him. So when Dr. Ace mentioned a graduate school word like *right*, implying achievement, my curiosity was awakened. I think that he was, so to speak, speaking my language of right and wrong and making up a theory to engage me. He is truly brilliant at this. Just when I think that I've had the last word and that I am absolutely right, or that I have left no stone unturned, he can come around with an even more accurate understanding. This is his clever way of engaging me, for I am more concerned with doing things right than having the right answer. Dr. Ace knows this about me and uses his insights on my behalf.

So perhaps it was slightly manipulative for him to say, "The right way or best way to conduct your second analysis is for you to lie on the couch." Or perhaps he was just right. In any case, I complied because he so rarely made suggestions. I had tried it before. I would try it again if this was the best approach.

Dr. Ace was right; because as soon as I lay on his couch, I was able to get in touch with scary feelings that were not available to me when I sat up. I immediately felt a funny pain in my pelvis. I was amazed and very ashamed of the feelings that were so easily brought up, feelings that I had forgotten were mine. Sometimes I was totally scared of my feelings, and especially the physical pain. It was very difficult to tell Dr. Ace that I had feelings of pain in my pelvis. Just getting the words out was an enormous emotional risk. But I also know that the pain and the talking about my other feelings had helped me to get a grip on my intellectual defenses, which quickly put these forms of self-protection or denial in their proper perspective.

Sitting here calmly, but not dispassionately, writing about this experience of enlightenment about my denial or my intellectual defenses seems somewhat hypocritical. It was really difficult for me to get to a point where I could trust that my feelings were as important as my ideas about what I should and should not do. But because the physical pain in my pelvis continued to be present and continued to be very difficult to talk about with Dr. Ace, I was convinced that I needed to turn to my feelings. It took a long time, almost a year of my second analysis, before I eventually developed enough confidence in my sense of self to be able to rethink my sense of failure in my analysis with Dr. Z. I was able to imagine talking to Dr. Z as if I were an equal partner in our analytic experience. I was aware that I had deeper problems that had not been explored in my first analysis. I was not aware exactly what these deeper problems were at that time. My memories of physical pain still faded in and out of my awareness.

Speaking up for myself with Dr. Z took a lot of courage. I had to face failure, an enormously difficult and humiliating experience for me, even though I had been treated as a failure my whole life. I had to be realistic, to accept that everything that goes wrong is not my fault, unlike the cruel lesson I had learned all too well as a child and relearned in my first analytic experience.

Dr. Ace helped me to reach the point where I felt able to confront Dr. Z, although I really wanted Dr. Ace to call Dr. Z for me. I even offered to give him my written permission, but Dr. Ace said it was neither in my best interest nor necessary for him to call. But he never told me to do it myself. He **never** said, "Confront Dr. Z with your anger and disappointment!" He waited until I felt entitled to my feelings of rage and despair, which he repeatedly indicated were understandable and unfortunate.

I can still remember how I thought I would never be able to confront the seemingly well-meaning and tragic Dr. Z. There was so much unresolved negative transference (he still made me feel bad about myself) and just plain bad feelings that I literally felt I could not speak up. But I was underestimating my conviction and courage. Eventually I did call Dr. Z. I said that I needed to talk with him. On the phone, he seemed busy and uninterested and did not really want to make an appointment with me. Dr. Ace kept reminding me that my investment should adaptively and appropriately be in my own need to discuss the past and to talk with Dr. Z. I had to call Dr. Z several times before we could find a time to talk. When we did find time to meet, Dr. Z told me that it was a free consultation. Now I wish that I could get *all my money back*.

The reality was that Dr. Z was not interested in hearing about my feelings. Still, it was difficult to accept his disinterest in me. Actually, it was unbelievable that I had worked so closely with him for so many years and he didn't even want to talk to me. Yet, it was *understandable* to Dr. Ace, who pointed out that this reluctance was just another indication of a bad match between patient and psychoanalyst. At that point even he didn't know the whole truth—of how bad the whole experience had been.

On some level I wanted to rip Dr. Ace's eyes out for being so logical and smart. How could he know about Dr. Z's defensive structure or his way of coping with uncomfortable feelings? He had never been in treatment with Dr. Z. But he knew more than

I did about Dr. Z. I had wasted all those years with Dr. Z. I could have resented Dr. Ace for knowing more than I did or I could have felt totally moronic; thankfully, I was able to appreciate his insight and to go on. Dr. Ace helped me to accept his point of view by not being critical of me. He also believed that I could handle his insights.

Dr. Ace was in a difficult situation. He did not want to be perceived as dispassionate or cold. Repeatedly, he asked me, "Do you think that I am being dispassionate?" In comparison to me, he was calmer than the deep blue sea. And I know it wouldn't have helped me if he were as infuriated as I was. I was infuriated with Dr. Z for trying to ignore me after I had spent so many years in analysis with him and had sacrificed my well-being for his well-being. Dr. Ace again calmly pointed out to me our different personality structures. When threatened, Dr. Z shut down and ignored other people's emotional input. I, on the other hand, took responsibility for everyone's problems when something went wrong. He was right again. Dr. Z and I were simply mismatched as patient and therapist. I had simply wasted ten years of work and too much money. I knew this was a bottom-line truth.

This was a horrifying insight. That the defensive structures of myself and Dr. Z were mismatched is one clear and serious reason why I am writing this book, for I am sure that most patients don't analyze their therapist's personality structure before they slowly and cautiously pour out their hearts and souls. Or, more simply stated, how can you decide if you have the doctor who will have your best interests at heart? How can you know if your therapist can admit to his or her own blind spots? How can you know if you are a patient or a victim?

Patients should not have to analyze their therapists' coping strategies. Therapists need to do this for themselves. Therapists need to know how their limitations affect their clients, not vice versa. This was the second hardest lesson that I have ever learned. The worst pain was that I was a victim of incest. Financially, it was the most expensive lesson that I had to learn. I hope that other people reading about my experiences will save themselves from both the intense emotional pain and the substantial financial loss that I suffered at the hands of Dr. Z.

*   *   *

It was quite an emotional accomplishment for me to talk to Dr. Z in person. It took me a year and a half to get up the emotional courage. When I did it, it was easy to keep my wits about me. Despite my fears, I was calm. I told Dr. Z that I had gone back into analysis with Dr. Ace. Dr. Z approved of him. In fact, he had to be a gossip and say that his own wife and someone else's wife, whom I knew very well, had been in analysis with Dr. Ace. I think that he said this to make me feel diminished, as if I were just another analyst's wife who was back in therapy with the doctor's wife's analyst. He knew that I hated being treated as an analyst's wife. He definitely acted in bad taste. But he didn't succeed in making me feel bad about myself. I just felt really sick inside. Dr. Z simply reaffirmed my sense that he could not, or would not, take responsibility for what damage he had done to my psychological growth and development. He didn't say, "I'm sorry. I used your compassion to ease my own pain."

I maintained my composure. I learned that Dr. Z had gone back into analysis to deal with the death of his daughter. I was relieved that he was getting the help that he needed. I learned that he was still a very judgmental, defensive, and critical person. I talked a little about my anger. He was, I hope, able to hear me and feel something about the tragedy of our work. Overall, there were no surprises and no miracles. Dr. Z was a kind, well-meaning man who needed to be in control of his feelings and my feelings. The ramifications of his approach could have been lethal for me. He had no apparent interest in understanding my feelings. He had wanted to understand my psychodynamics or my role in the family. Sadly, and unfortunately,

I was to learn, in spite of his intellectual focus on my childhood, he had missed an important and extremely crucial dynamic from my family life. He had not uncovered the most crucial traumatic experiences in my life. He had never suspected that I was sexually abused.

*   *   *

The painful outcome of my confrontation with Dr. Z was extremely difficult for me to accept. In all honesty, it was emotionally devastating to realize that I had gone for help and instead I had been seriously hurt. I had hurt my family in turn by accepting my negative diagnosis of being overemotional and oversensitive—I had been led astray on my journey to self-understanding. I was farther from knowing myself than I had been when I first met Dr. Z.

When I got beyond feeling overwhelmed by my pain, I was enlightened, which freed me to look deeper into my past. I am still impressed with the irony of this painful situation.

*   *   *

Dr. Z would definitely take more responsibility for his actions about his negligent treatment than my brother was ever able to concede to or even acknowledge about his abusive treatment of me. But Dr. Z and I somehow played that old childhood game with each other. I tried to take on every challenge that he prescribed without getting burned. I was emotionally out on a ledge looking down at my own self-destruction when I left therapy. I had been victimized by Dr. Z's judgmentality. This reality was extremely difficult to acknowledge personally and professionally. The feelings of betrayal are still painful, though I now understand them and see them in perspective.

FIVE

Recovering Forgotten Memories

I am not overgeneralizing when I say that no one wants to be betrayed or victimized. Betrayal is a dreadful and powerful experience that is always difficult to accept because it implies a broken trust that is made mutually and in good faith. Betrayal and victimization imply disappointment and misunderstanding. Betrayal in psychoanalysis or psychotherapy is a serious problem that creates confusion and chaos for the more vulnerable member of the therapeutic pair. Victimization in psychoanalysis is like disfigurement in surgery. If the knife slips in the surgeon's hand, the patient may suffer serious consequences, even death. If a therapist underestimates or overestimates the patient's capacity, there are also serious ramifications for emotional and intellectual well-being of the patient. Serious betrayal and victimization are always psychological experiences for women and men who have been sexually abused, making the therapeutic encounter potentially more dangerous or extremely healing for them.

My own experience of feeling betrayed and victimized by my first analyst was extremely difficult for me to accept emotionally and intellectually because I am a therapist myself. But perhaps I idealize the profession as well. Feeling betrayed by Dr. Z was overwhelmingly painful. Even writing about my experience now, I still remember the shock and confusion. How did this happen to me? I have gone over this question many times, even though I know the answers. I still feel sick to my stomach when I think of the emotional and financial investment that ended up being so extremely wasteful and hurtful. I feel sorry and sad for myself as well as for my husband and my children because we were all hurt. We were all betrayed. I know that the psychological research shows that my family and I are not alone (Bass & Davis, 1988; Blume, 1989; Frederickson, 1992).

As I write down these words, I feel compelled to say that Dr. Z was well-meaning and, as Dr. Ace says, "It was unfortunate." I don't think Dr. Z set out to hurt me. I think that he still believes he helped me. Nevertheless, and in spite of his well-meaning approach, I was betrayed by his limited vision of psychoanalysis and his own limitations as an analyst. He tried and he failed, and I got abused. *It has taken me a long time to get that straight.* I used to think that he betrayed me because I was a bad, worthless person. As my sense of defectiveness and resulting sense of shame have diminished, I no longer believe this. My belief system is common for individuals who have been sexually abused (Miller, 1983, 1984, 1988).

My not taking responsibility for Dr. Z's limitations, accepting that I was betrayed and victimized, has helped me personally and professionally. It has enhanced my confidence and my self-esteem. It has also allowed me to look deeper into my past and understand the roots of my depression and the perception of myself as bad. I would never advise anyone to take this route of betrayal to self-understanding. I know that I did this the hard way and that I have serious regrets and enormous rage.

*   *   *

Ironically, my enlightenment about the atrocities of my early life came out of my rage at Dr. Z.

When I lay down on Dr. Ace's couch and began talking about

my associations with my childhood experiences, my first reaction was to believe I was the bad twin because I had been chosen to be sexually abused. Suddenly I felt pain in my lower pelvis. Again my immediate association was that it was my fault that "they" sexually exploited me. Even though I have no singular memory of an event, it was just this feeling in my body that I got in touch with as I talked with Dr. Ace about my limited childhood memories. I learned in my quest for knowledge about sexual abuse that often the first memories of childhood sexual abuse are physical (Frederickson, 1992; Perlman, 1992, 1993).

My first reaction to this insight about possible sexual abuse was outrage at Dr. Z. Of course, I thought that if I had been the therapist, I would have suspected sexual abuse. Perhaps I might see a woman with symptoms and a psychological history similar to my own for two or three months before making the diagnosis. Many books and much research are available to help the clinician make a diagnosis of sexual abuse. Dr. Z had more than enough time and more than enough information about my childhood to suspect sexual abuse, yet he did not. Dr. Ace was able to see the problem immediately. He trusted that my feelings and my physical pain were real symptoms of my past traumatic experiences.

Why hadn't Dr. Z considered sexual abuse? I was infuriated. I thought, "What an idiot!" Or "How oblivious can someone be?" I asked my husband what he thought. Like me he was infuriated and resented Dr. Z. Being a well-trained analyst, my husband offered me the following theory: "Dr. Z was unconsciously in love with you, and he could not consider that you had been treated this way by anyone." My husband went on about how this conscious or unconscious countertransference feeling of love for me determined how he dealt with me throughout the entire analysis. I think my husband's theory is more than adequate, but it doesn't calm me down to know this interpretation. It doesn't get Dr. Z off the hook with me. And sometimes it really doesn't help to understand. There are times when I just feel infuriated that I was used, first by my father and brother and then by my analyst. I appreciate my husband's insights only when I am in a calmer state of mind.

Dr. Ace knew that I was possessed by the need to know what happened to me, and he began calmly thinking with me about my early experiences. He really gave it his all. He never said that I was too far out or making up stories. He never implied that I was just fantasizing, as might a Freudian analyst (Freud, 1921; Perlman, 1993). He believed in me even though I myself sometimes felt as if I were making up these traumatic experiences, because I had feelings of unreality about the whole experience.

Dr. Ace could not work fast enough for me, although I am always amazed at how much we do get done in each session. I do not think he was avoiding the issue; I simply wanted my memories back. I wanted to understand quickly, and I wanted to make up for lost time. In short, what I wanted was a miracle, and Dr. Ace was wise enough to know that psychoanalysis was a lot of work and not a miracle.

Still, I was insistent to remember the details of the sexual abuse. I called my twin sister to see if she remembered sexual exploitation. She could not recall anything specific, but she agreed that our brother was, in her words, evil enough to do anything. She thought the abuse was possible, but at first she wasn't as upset about the possibility as I was, although her reaction changed drastically over time. She tried to help me by composing possible scenarios. We went over our possible shared memories. Clearly, she remembered more than I did of our past. I filed that idea in my computerized brain hoping that it would lead to the clue that would help me remember.

I really wanted to be able to break through the amnesia surrounding my childhood memories. Remembering became my unstated goal, my mission in life. I was so totally shocked to know that I had "forgotten memories" that might be crucial to understanding myself. Why hadn't Dr. Z thought about why I had become the bad twin when I was younger? It would, I thought, have been easier to access these memories before I developed my strong propensity to theorize and intellectualize about my experiences. In other words, I was worried, and rightly so, that I was too old to remember and that my memories and my feelings had been made harder to access by my first analysis. I knew that I had gotten farther from the truth, not closer.

It was at this time that I developed a strong dislike for general analytic interpretations. Dr. Z's interpretation that my mother was limited as a parent and that in her mind she split my sister and me into good and bad in order to relate to us was only a bargain-basement vision of my childhood. There were more to my childhood experiences than this seemingly inclusive, yet shallow and one-dimensional interpretation. But Dr. Z had been satisfied with this understanding and didn't wish to go deeper. Nor did I question his judgment, for he was the doctor, and by my history I was unconsciously seduced into compliance. The young child does not question her father when he says, "I am sure you will like lying down beside me."

After my anger subsided with Dr. Z, I had to face the seriousness of my problem. I knew that I had been sexually abused, but I had very few memories to rely on. I had to realize that actually remembering my past traumatic experiences was going to be an entirely different experience than wanting to remember them. I had to realize that I could not make my memory come back. I had to realize also that my first analysis had created more repression, not less. I had to deal with the feeling of darkness and confusion that comes with amnesia. I had to deal with the feeling of unreality that is evoked from knowing that I did not know. And I had to accept that I had been seriously traumatized. I learned to live with only my clues. I learned to see either only a part of the picture, so very unreal and so very strange, or I would have to deny my sensibility. Both options, the sense of darkness, trauma, and confusion or the denial, were scary for me. I knew that I had to face my past even though it was really confusing and unsettling for me. My past would not go away. It haunted me, as much as I was programmed or trained to ignore it.

At this point my second analysis began to work for me in a profound way. With Dr. Ace I had to go over and over what could have happened. He wanted me to remember what I had repressed. The difference between his perspective and my own was crucial. I was determined to remember. Although Dr. Ace thought it was critical for me to remember, he accepted that with or without concrete memories, I had been sexually abused. In fact, he thought that sexual abuse was only one of several forms of abuse I had suffered at the hands of my father and brother.

Intellectually I could appreciate his point of view, but my emotional curiosity would overwhelm me. My experiences of trying to remember and not being able to remember were powerfully unnerving. Oftentimes I felt out of control of my life because of the holes in my own self-understanding. Even though Dr. Ace strongly encouraged me not to try too hard to remember, I was obsessed with remembering. I was driven.

Dr. Ace and I examined my phobias in detail. I have always been terrified of fish. Dr. Z had thought this was based on some "archaic fear" and dismissed it. Dr. Ace and I tried to understand my fear of fish—to take it seriously—as perhaps as a representation of my fear of early childhood sexual abuse. *I remember that we went on a fishing vacation at Bass Lake, near Yosemite National Park. We stayed in cabins, and I was afraid of this fish my father and brother cooked in the frying pan. I refused to eat the fish, and I still cannot eat fish. That's all I remember, but I still feel terrified of those fish looking up at me in the frying pan.* I wonder what else happened at that cabin in the woods that I cannot remember. My mother remembered my fish phobia, and connected this phobia to my brother's goldfish, which died when my brother was younger. I do not remember my brother's goldfish at all.

There is another clue, which my mother talked with me about in recent years. She said that when I was younger, from age four to about nine, I always had earaches. I remember one or two, but I do not remember having them continually. My mother said that my brother used to lie in bed with me, and that this is what *helped* my earaches. He was the only one who could comfort me, she said. Clearly, my brother would get in bed with me, and this, my mother indicated, would make me feel better. I know now from recovered memories that my brother would get in bed with me and masturbate himself and me.

The other clue about incestuous experiences comes solely from my own memories of hotel rooms and cabins. Terrified of strange-looking run-down hotels and cabins, I refuse to stay in them. I become terrified just thinking of being alone in a run-down hotel room. I just cannot do it. I do not know why. My mother says that we used to go down to San Diego and go camping and visit our paternal grandmother, but I do not remember these trips. Yet I believe the fear of hotel rooms is related to these visits and whatever happened in these rooms and at Yosemite. I am still afraid of run-down hotels and motels.

What is really fascinating to me is that my mother could talk very openly with me about my brother and my earaches, my fish phobia, and our family trips, yet I was terrified of talking with her about them. My mother seemed eager to want to help me to remember, but emotionally I could not accept her openness even though I knew it would be good for me to speak more openly with her. Her courage in trying to help me remember what I had forgotten was not enough to help me get in touch with what actually did happen. I am still afraid to remember all the painful details of the abuse. As Dr. Ace points out to me, the details are still too painful to come into my awareness, although many repressed memories surfaced as I worked on writing this book.

*   *   *

Understanding that the betrayal I experienced in my first analysis was a reenactment of the abuse I experienced as a child was easier for me to understand intellectually than for me to feel, tolerate, and accept as an emotional experience. In other words, as the picture of my first analysis was sketched in with feelings, facts, and associations, I was able to think about my vulnerability to abuse and exploitation. But experiencing the scary feelings that were evoked when I realized that I was so readily vulnerable to the demands of others was painful. I felt as if I had limited resources to draw upon when I needed to protect myself from the demands of significant others. I realized, as well, that thinking about what I needed from others was very hard for me to conceptualize and completely unfamiliar. Feeling entitled to my feelings was even more difficult.

My lack of connection to my feelings explains why at first my associations and the feelings I talked about with Dr. Ace seemed so foggy or transparent. I was just not used to making my feelings important or real. When I was a child, my feelings were always treated as secondary to my sister's, my father's, or my brother's. Later my feelings were treated by Dr. Z as troublesome to his sense of how I should be. Thus even my first analyst did not respect my feelings. He respected instead my capacity to achieve, to think things through, to follow orders. This was a repetition of my childhood experience.

No one had ever taken my feelings at face value before I met Dr. Ace. My husband and my children had their own interests in perceiving my feelings as important or not important, depending on the situation. More simply, motherhood and marriage in your twenties is not conducive to developing a firm sense of entitlement. Mothers are often by necessity selfless. Doctors' wives have to learn that other people can interrupt their time with their husband. I was able to adapt quickly to the selfless role of good mother and compassionate doctor's wife.

Sadly for me, my feelings were ignored or put on the back burner. So when I had to focus on them, it was scary or strange and certainly unfamiliar. In some ways I found it difficult to believe that my feelings were ever important. Perhaps this is why I had such difficulties believing that I really had amnesia.

I could not believe what I felt about the darkness I saw when I closed my eyes. I was really afraid to think that something had happened to me that was so terrible that I did not want to remember.

In summary, the process of owning my negative feelings of anger, disappointment, betrayal, and victimization, as well as my positive feelings of self-worth, was a major part of my second analysis. Feeling entitled to my feelings led me to believe and then accept that I had amnesia in reaction to being sexually abused by my father and brother. I still lack total recall of events—just fragments of memories surface. I know that I was considered bad, because I was sexually abused: My father's and my brother's justification for abusing me was that I was bad, that I deserved to be used by them. Actually, as a child I was just totally helpless and vulnerable. As an adult, however, I am not helpless and vulnerable. I am not automatically subject to exploitation, though I suffered a form of exploitation in my first analysis. I am seriously concerned about the children who are likely to be abused and exploited as I was, as well as about adults who may have suffered a similar traumatic experience and need to deal with the aftereffects.

* * *

Today I do remember more than I did at the beginning of my analysis with Dr. Ace. Life seems more real. Not only can I remember details, but the details seem more real, more alive, and more meaningful. I feel more connected to my memories and my sensibility about being emotionally and sexually abused. I can talk more openly about the physical pain in my pelvis. And yet the truth is that I cannot remember in detail the events that led to my fear of fish and hotel rooms. But I am totally aware of my phobic reactions. I hope that someday I may remember more specifically what happened to me. I feel more at peace with myself about the empty spaces in my memory. I know that certain strategies have helped me to be more accepting and less ashamed that I was emotionally and sexually exploited. The primary tool in remembering has been my desire to remember and the persistent encouragement of Dr. Ace and my husband, children, mother, sister, and friends who have openly listened to me, believing in me and supporting me. That I am a psychotherapist and regularly hear about sexual abuse has helped me as well. Clearly, the exposure to children and other adults with similar traumatic experiences has made me feel less alone and less defective. Also listening to other people's life histories, including their experiences with amnesia, has helped me to feel less damaged.

Along with emotional support and acceptance from others has come my concrete sense that I do forget what I have done. I used to think that I was just absent-minded—like an absent-minded professor with his head in the clouds, oblivious to those more earthly details. To avoid forgetting, I always make lists. When a lot is going on, which is often, then I have my lists all over the place. The more anxious I feel, the more lists I make. When I am calm, however, I rarely forget.

Perhaps I am an absent-minded professor type, but more is involved in my memory problem than this. I can as easily forget the present as the past. This is an eerie experience. Consider this example of my total memory loss, which happens often: I drive over to Dr. Ace's office the same time four days a week. I rush up the stairs, as I am always busy and never really get to his office in time to look at magazines. I push the light switch, which tells him I have arrived. And then I *forget* that I have pushed the light. So I sit and count to 60, and if he opens his door, I know that I have pushed the light switch. But I do not remember actually pushing the switch. Even writing about this seems sickeningly strange. Such forgetting is a symptom left over from my childhood to remind me that I still have forgotten memories. *The symptoms are crucial*, for they indicate that there are more memories that I have unconsciously buried.

I rarely forget what I have to do for others; that is easier for me. I have a nearly photographic memory of important dreams and associations from my patients. I try to be in charge of what I have to do for my husband and my children. I am extremely organized and efficient in all other aspects of my personal and professional life. I just have these brief memory losses in relationships to things that I need to accomplish for myself. So I write lists to deal with the problem. And so I count the seconds as I wait for Dr. Ace to open his office door.

Dr. Ace works really hard to keep me focused on my memory loss or lapses while not making me feel ashamed or foolish. He says that I long for attention, then feel conflicted over getting attention, and then forget I want attention. To accept this interpretation on an emotional level was difficult. Perhaps getting attention was just too painful and convoluted, for attention was connected with sexual abuse and exploitation. I got more than I wanted or needed. As a result, I am afraid that when I connect with someone, I might get more than I bargained for. The other person might go too far. Then again, perhaps getting attention for myself takes away from what others need for themselves. This follows a familiar pattern, for it may be that I existed to support my sister, brother, and father and as a child felt I was not entitled to get what I wanted. I felt that I was not deserving.

* * *

Looking at my childhood experience in relationship to my forgotten memories has been enlightening. It has given me the ability to look at myself in a different way. Although it is extremely painful to think that I was so mistreated or exploited that there are things I cannot remember, the pain is really easier to bear than trying to be superwoman in order to avoid feeling bad about myself. To know the whole truth is more important than to understand only the symptoms and to try to cover them up or deny them, which is what I learned to do through achievement in my first analytic experience.

The difficult and painful experience of trying to get in touch with my forgotten memories has been crucial to my sense of self on both a personal and professional level. I feel better about myself and I know I am a more competent therapist because my analytic work now focuses on my amnesia and memory lapses.

As I end this chapter, I realize that it is a testament to the human spirit and to the people who care about me deeply that I have been able to identify more specifically the types of abuse that occurred in my early life. Trying to get in touch with my long-forgotten secret sexual relationships with my father and brother has been the hardest emotional experience I have ever attempted. For me incest was a well-hidden secret, a secret that was locked up behind the walls of my twinship and the structure of an upstanding orthodox Jewish family. It may be that some of the facts are too shielded with lies and deceit to be seen clearly, but my feelings have a life that reflects my true experience. I have come to believe my feelings and use them to help me sort through the lies and coverups that conveniently made my oppressors content with their own behavior and their treatment of me as a very young child and later as an adolescent and adult.

Why did my father and brother have to cover up the truth if they did not feel bad about what they did to me?

SIX

Developing a New Sense of Self

I had faced my despair about being sexually abused in order to develop a positive sense of myself. I couldn't run and hide from the pain or keep it a secret any longer. In actuality, I wondered how I could integrate this experience into my reality, my every-day functioning. How could I talk to other people about this experience? It was such a complicated issue for me. It was more than just a challenge, for a challenge means to me that there is a right or wrong decision to be made, a decision that can be evaluated objectively. There was no objectively correct way to handle my despair in the world outside of Dr. Ace's office. I had to take my own direction.

There were options. I have heard about other people through personal and professional conversations who have been injured or exploited by their therapists. Ethics committees exist to listen to these allegations from abused patients. These committees take action against people they deem to be negligent. I thought about this as a possibility, but I really didn't feel this was my best option. Dr. Z had been successful in treating me on many levels. I am an accomplished writer and a successful doctor. Other professionals would argue whether or not Dr. Z had failed. I myself wondered whether he had failed as a result of his treatment strategy or his perspective. In addition, I could never forget his tragedy and his loss. With the death of his daughter, he had suffered in a way that I hope I will never have to suffer. I can't imagine a more horrendous tragedy than losing a daughter. Suing him for malpractice was absurd in light of the circumstances, and I was not willing to take my problems in front of an ethics committee or into a court of law. I believed, and still do believe, that doing this would seriously distort my experiences and my pain. In other words, this wasn't just an ethical issue or a financial loss. Here was a tragedy. It was as Dr. Ace so beautifully stated, "unfortunate" that Dr. Z and I had worked together as analyst and patient.

Dealing with the aftermath of the tragedy was complicated. Everyone had been injured. Dr. and Mrs. Z had lost their daughter. I had suffered a serious betrayal and ensuing depression. My children and my husband had been neglected in insidious ways. I am sure that my professional life also suffered. But Dr. Z was clearly a tragic victim as well. Getting back at him through a meeting of some ethics committee seemed meaningless. What would I have gained by humiliating him in front of his peers? Would he pay the bills for my second analysis? Was it worth it? Would I feel better? Would that really accomplish anything? The answer was always no. I felt that I had to take responsibility for the problem in my own way. I didn't want some ethics board or a lawyer to do what I needed to do for myself. I wanted to use my own voice.

I decided what I needed to do was to write about my experiences to understand about the power and destructiveness of the therapeutic process, especially from the viewpoint of a survivor of sexual abuse. This was a difficult decision to make. I knew I would be exposing a very vulnerable part of myself to others who could and would easily judge me as defective. On some level I was afraid to let people know me so profoundly. The reactions of my husband, my children, my mother, and my sister concerned me. I didn't want anyone to get hurt again. There was enough damage to deal with already. I worried about my patients and my husband's patients. Should they know me in such a personal way? Should they be subjected to my personal saga? What would my colleagues think? Some people will say that writing this story for everyone to read is unethical. I didn't want to be provocative, but I didn't want to ignore my despair. I wanted to be a survivor, not a victim.

At the end of my reflections about the ramifications of my experience, I started writing about what had happened. I found out that writing was a way to face my despair and the potential despair of others. The act of writing was an effective way to try to gain insight into the problem of betrayal in psychoanalysis and the question of effective treatment of sexual abuse. How other people react to my decision to write seems a serious, but secondary concern. In short, I am not oblivious to the provocativeness of my written words and other people's reactions to me, but now my feelings focus on what *I* need to attend to— worrying about others would be a detour at this point in my life. However, being at this crossroad is not easy, and I often feel anxious about exposing such personal issues to people who don't want to understand them and who lack compassion.

In the past, writing has always helped me to feel better about myself because it puts my ideas and feelings in perspective. Writing about my sense of despair over my first analysis, in which my incestuous experiences were not explored, has effectively allowed me to develop a better sense of myself. Writing has made me feel less ashamed and less isolated with the problem. It has given me hope that I may be able to enlighten or assist other people who are in similar "betrayal potential" situations in their own lives. Instead of withdrawing into shame, I am trying to connect to others who are also at risk. This feels right. My intent is *not* to humiliate Dr. Z, but to explore a problem that remains hidden to the consumers of psychoanalysis and psychotherapy.

* * *

There are other facets of my recovery, my growing self-understanding, besides the cure of writing about it. I no longer feel depressed or self-sacrificing or unimportant. I feel important to others; indeed, I know I am important to others. I think that two insights from my psychoanalytic work with Dr. Ace have facilitated my renewed sense of value as a person. First, knowing and feeling that I was treated as bad or defective, because I was sexually abused, has made my life more understandable. In other words, it has been more psychologically comforting to realize that a traumatic event or events occurred that gave me this negative identity than to perceive myself as the projection of the bad part of my mother. And as horrifying as considering that I was sexually abused has been, it does make sense to me. I can understand my own phobic reactions as coming from specific events, instead of as forms of "irrational craziness."

Although accepting the reality of sexual abuse has been frightening, I feel calmer in general. I can understand my reactions as coming from somewhere within myself. I feel less anxious and less overreactive. For example, if I know I am afraid of hotel rooms for a reason, I can deal with the fear, but if I just have a vague and diffuse dislike that I try to dismiss as a sign of being a spoiled "Jewish princess," then I am continually belittling myself and never getting the chance to understand why I am so upset.

Put another way, Dr. Z couldn't understand why I was treated as if I were bad. His psychological explanation—that it was convenient for my mother, based on her own limitations, to see me as bad and my sister as good—was psychologically incomplete, inaccurate, and ultimately destructive. Dr. Z felt I would always be subject to depression and certain phobic reactions. How wrong again! Dr. Ace was more open minded. He was sure that we could understand both the extent and the basis of my depression. And we have done that together. Even though there are holes in my memories, I know enough to be sure that my depression comes from traumatically induced exploitation at a early age, not from a diffuse depressive nature.

I have come to feel that I have control when I feel depressed. As a result, I don't get depressed as easily. Based on an understanding of events, I know what makes me feel more distraught. I know what is terrifying, overwhelming, or just not good for me. I know why. My depression seems more like an allergic reaction to certain stimuli than a foreboding that hangs over my head and that is unmanageable.

The second insight that has markedly and distinctly improved my sense of self has been my ability to elaborate and understand in detail the meaning of the memory of playing hot foot or footsie with my brother and sister. Dr. Z was able to see how self-destructive this game was to my sense of self, but we never delved into the ramifications of this game in the development of my driven personality. In fact, Dr. Z encouraged me to act out the game in real life. I was always taking on too much work and feeling pressured. Dr. Z never asked, "Why so many books? Why so many Ph.D.s?" Why did he not ask me why I was so driven? I wonder, did it help him feel more successful because I was able to achieve? I can only speculate that he felt that my achievements meant that his treatment with me was going well.

I don't know why he didn't see that the feelings associated with this concrete but symbolic experience were essential to the way I organized myself psychologically. It is one thing to know that you are acting overly successful and very brave and that this behavior is overdetermined by the past, but it is really quite another to experience yourself acting this behavior out and trying to control it in your life. For me to understand how my behavior related to my childhood game of footsie with my sister and brother was therefore crucial to my recovery.

What I am trying to say is that *intellectual insight is very limited if it is not applied to your emotional life*. So when I ended psychoanalysis with Dr. Z, I knew intellectually that I was driven and why. I knew that high achievement was my only way to feel better about myself—or to not feel bad about myself. But I didn't know how to stop pushing myself to write more books, to see more patients, to be a better wife and a better mother. I was still driven to do what "I should do and what I should be" in order to feel good about myself. I knew why this was overdetermined by my childhood experiences, but it didn't help me to stop. I was still totally focused on the idea of what I should be. And in this way I was still tied to my abusive and exploitive father and brother. I could never do something for myself that didn't meet other people's approval. Understanding the addiction to work as a way to boost my self-esteem and trying to set limits wasn't enough. It actually just made me feel more frustrated and more empty and isolated from the world.

What helped was when I talked with Dr. Ace about the emotional experience of having those matches placed between my toes. We talked about the associated feeling states and of trying too hard to deny my feelings. I realized that I was always playing this game. This was the only psychological way for me to exist. I would take on a challenge that might on some level be self-destructive to my own sense of safety. I wouldn't get hurt because I was too smart. But it took its toll on my ability to function. For example, a colleague might need a test report completed. It might take me 20 hours to complete. I would say yes and do the work without considering how it might jeopardize my own emotional stability and personal happiness. I would rather feel harassed and overwhelmed than just say no, because to say no meant that I wasn't playing the game of life; to say no was a challenge that jeopardized my psychic existence, even though I knew that nothing would happen, that I would get more referrals and I would still be able to pay my rent. Other people would understand no as a sign of being human; for them it is okay to say, "I'm sorry, I can't do that for you." But for me, it brought up horrible feelings of dread and anxiety, a fear of alienation and abandonment. What would happen if I didn't play this game? What would happen if I didn't want to set myself up to get burned? Why was this game my best option?

I know the game was a reaction to some traumatic event. I believe that I did say no to someone significant, and I really regretted having given up or given in. I never developed a sense that it was okay to say no. In most situations I was exploited emotionally or sexually for the other person's pleasure. Compliance was a mandatory requirement of my childhood. I learned that to say no was more traumatic than to give in to the abuse. It continues to horrify me to think that speaking up for myself was *not* an option.

Compliance to Dr. Z's treatment plan became understandable to me, given the parameters of my early life. I am not confusing "understandable" with "okay" or "justified." Clearly, asking me to comply with what Dr. Z saw as in my own best interest was counterproductive because it just reenacted my need to be compliant in the transference relationship established between us. My compliance to others should have been interpreted, not enacted. Had I understood the roots of my compliance, perhaps my memories of childhood would have been more accessible. I can never know the answer to this speculation. I can only surmise that this may have been a much easier route to self-understanding.

* * *

Dealing with the aftermath means facing my regrets about what might have been had I seen Dr. Ace first and never met up with Dr. Z. One way to put the experience into perspective was to write about it, and in writing about it I must add that on a philosophical level people learn from their painful experiences, often allowing them to become more courageous and humane. I think that I am a much wiser therapist because of this experience. As a result I can more patiently accept the limitations of other people with whom I work. In addition, I am less critical of myself and my own mistakes. I am more watchful of being hurt and absorbing the pain. I am also extremely careful about not doing to others what was done to me.

* * *

I have learned to protect myself from other people's remarks. I have learned to value my own limits as legitimate and important to me and to others. I have learned that my selflessness could easily backfire into depression. I have learned that there were advantages for everyone around me, including myself, when I didn't feel depressed. In learning these things I have made progress on the road to recovery.

Once I began to protect myself from overwork and overstimulation from others by not acting like a supersponge, I felt better. When the word *no* became an invaluable or golden option, I was able to slow down. Slowing down while still maintaining my self-esteem was a difficult challenge and a welcome victory. It took many, many years, however. Emotionally it was difficult to stop playing footsie. I was afraid to slow down and to say no, even when I knew that reality dictated this reaction. I had to accept my past and recognize that its requirements were not the requirements of my adulthood. Dr. Ace and I worked carefully and long to get me to stop taking every challenge that came along. I had to know that my existence was important when I was passive. I still regress, still act out my need to put myself under extreme pressure and not get burned. This is a continual challenge for me, and it is entirely different from just getting involved in a challenge because it is a familiar experience or because it makes me feel alive and safe and not afraid to be unchallenged.

Dr. Ace's prescription for overcoming my excessive need to excel continues to be that I follow my own inclinations or feelings. I have learned to think first about what feels good or positive to me and not to worry about what others expect from me, about what I should do, about what I could do. Dr. Ace has really encouraged me to reflect on the differences between the "should do's," the "could do's," and the actions I actually desire and need to take in my life.

Should is the malignant word in my vocabulary, says Dr. Ace, and that's a very strong statement coming from behind the couch. I take this idea seriously even though the old transference feelings from my father and brother can interfere with my reflections and make me fearful to say no. Thus sometimes when

I am overwhelmed, I fear that if I say no I will be humiliated or exploited. Saying no has become more natural for me, nonetheless.

In conclusion, I believe that the aftermath of my first analysis and the aftermath of my childhood are directly related to each other. *The conscious and sometimes unconscious symptoms I suffer from result from the fear of not being compliant.* This is the emotional aftermath, the symptom manifest in my personality that I consciously try not to act out. In other words, it is not natural or comfortable for me to just say, "No, I can't do that for you." I believe that this is a legacy for all abused individuals.

SEVEN

Forgotten Memories

I have always been self-conscious and obsessed with remembering what is happening in my life. Sometimes I have an almost photographic memory; at other times I forget what I have just completed. I forget when I feel overwhelmed, confused, or conflicted. Forgetting or remembering is a serious, pervasive issue for me that manifests itself in various ways in my life.

I wish I could feel more comfortable about my problem with forgetting and just accept it for what it is. It is, after all, totally dysfunctional to be so vigilant about what is happening next. I know that I make the problem of forgetting more serious in reality than it really is or needs to be. What happens to me, I believe, is that I get preoccupied with other events in my life and then I simply become absent-minded, which is not so serious.

The real problem is my emotional reaction to forgetting, which I experience as an extremely *bad thing to do*. Falsely believing that I am remembering everything except my past protects me from feeling panicky and preoccupied with the past. This is a totally irrational and defensive way of approaching my life, but my defenses function to help me feel safe from experiencing something I might have to block out of my memory again.

This problem extends to my family as well. For example, I ask my children every day I see them, "What's up?" They sometimes think that I am "uptight" because I always have to know what is "up" to feel organized. I trust my children to make good decisions. Is my obsession with knowing what will happen and protecting myself from harm just a bad habit left over from childhood? In fact, people who just meet me can pick up easily how panicky I can get with the unknown and with disorganization; and if they are kind, they try to be reassuring. This is how Dr. Z tried to connect with me. He wanted to calm me down and reassure me. Dr. Z figured out that I needed my life to be very clear and understandable. He tried to help me calm down instead of trying to understand why I needed so much order. Dr. Z failed in his approach and betrayed me because he didn't understand and interpret the transference and countertransference issues related to being in control. Instead, he acted out his countertransference by reassuring me. Predicting my future was an enactment of his own omnipotence, his countertransference. Instead, what I really needed to know about myself was why I felt that everything had to be in order all the time. What were the underlying issues in my psyche that created the need to be so much in control? Why did I feel so vulnerable when I felt in need of attention from someone that it was nearly impossible to ask for that attention directly?

I believe that as a young child growing up, I never received the right kind of attention. I was either exploited, overstimulated, or ignored. I found that being ignored by acting in control of myself at all times was far safer than showing my vulnerabilities. When I was vulnerable, I was subject to some form of humiliation. Instead of helping me to understand my fear of vulnerability, Dr. Z helped me act as if I were in control.

Now I can tolerate disorganization better because I am no longer vulnerable to the abuse and chaos of my childhood. My children, my husband, Dr. Ace, my sister, and friends who are very close to me are organized and responsible adults who are tuned into my feelings. But because of my own conscious and unconscious preoccupation with order and memory and an enormous fear of vulnerability, I feel that I need to know what is going on in my life all the time. I need to protect myself from getting into a situation I might not be able to tolerate. My vigilance about not forgetting and feeling confused is distressing and confusing for me and everyone around me. I am aware that this is how I let others understand that my past is still alive. The vulnerability I experienced was totally traumatic. Thus on some level I want to avoid the terror of feeling that my life is disorganized.

Despite all I understand intellectually, it is startling to me how distressed I can get when my life gets disorganized. I can still be overwhelmed by the unknown, although Dr. Ace's analysis has helped me to lessen this symptom. I believe this fear of disorganization is related to a reccurring dream that I had for the first several years of my second analysis. In this dream picture, *I am walking in a forest talking with my twin sister, and we are happy and playing. Then, unexpectedly, she lets go of my hand and gives me to a doctor who scares me. I can't remember what the doctor does to me, but I wake up terrified.* I do remember that as a child my brother played doctor with me.

I believe this dream picture is a childhood screen memory about incestuous experiences in my childhood. My nightmares led me to believe that my sister was not with me when I was abused. She was my protector, but she was not strong enough to keep me from getting hurt. I also believe that I was chosen to be the victim and that this made my sister feel defective as well, since she was not chosen but was trapped into allying with my brother.

I know that when I began my analysis with Dr. Z, *I was having terrible nightmares about someone coming to my bedroom trying to kill me.* At that time I was often alone, because my husband was working late at the hospital as a medical student. These night terrors persisted for over 20 years until I realized that I had been sexually abused. Once I understood what had happened to me, the nightmares began to fade away.

I know the reasons for organization and control in my life are no longer necessary. When life gets chaotic, I have to work with myself not to get panicky. I consciously try not to get negative, reminding myself that I know that my life is not conducive to order. After all, I am in a helping profession that works from a crisis-oriented perspective. I don't believe that I can read Tarot cards and predict the future. I am not an accountant, whose job is to help others bring order to their lives. My job is to understand the emotional issues of my clients.

Intellectually, I am opposed to order. I actually find very meticulous people, houses, cars, and offices offensive aesthetically. I like the disheveled and offbeat look. And yet keeping my memories in order is psychologically critical to me, so that I still have to work hard when things look or feel disorganized. These are the leftovers of my abusive and chaotic childhood.

*   *   *

My obsession with my memories is real, based on memories I have forgotten or repressed. I cannot as yet allow myself to consciously remember all the details of traumatic situations in my childhood, but I can accept this reality and I no longer feel an obsession to remember everything as I did when I was first aware of the amnesia. Memories continue to come back into my mind as if they had never been taken away from my conscious awareness.

*   *   *

Primarily, what I can still not remember visually are the extremely traumatic experiences, such as all the times my brother got in bed with me and the various types of abuse that I experienced at Bass Lake or the hotels that I stayed in as a young child with my father and brother. Recently, my memories about the attic stairs at my father's drug store have surfaced. Lost frightening memories are like a white light of terror for me. Joyful memories of good times past that are gone and forgotten make me feel sad because those good times are over. Like memories of your first rose or your first love, they are gone from conscious

awareness. And this is a loss, nevertheless. But there is a fond-
ness and a longing for the lost connection with these feelings,
which can be recaptured by an emotional stimulus that is evoc-
ative or by reminders from others.

Forgotten memories of traumatic events are terrifying. There
is a sense of annihilation connected with them, a sense that the
individual feels psychically or emotionally annihilated and can't
remember because he or she did not exist emotionally at the
time of the incident. The emotional and intellectual life of the
victim was crushed by the will of the perpetrator. The tragedy
is perhaps that the memory really never existed for the individual
being abused because the victim didn't really exist in a psychological sense. Now this may sound like a rarified and philosophical abstract concept, but this is the way I understand the
experience related to extreme traumatic experiences that create
temporary or partial amnesia, whether visual or emotional (Ulman & Brothers, 1988).

My understanding comes from my own experiences and from
other patients' descriptions of their traumatic experiences. My
sense of the white light—of the terror of amnesia that comes
from the lack of visual or emotional memory—is that the experience is objective or concretely real. The person did not exist
psychologically because of the intrusiveness of the abuser. There
is a sense that the victims feel disconnected from themselves.
In reality, they did not exist. Their subjective sense of self was
obliterated by the traumatic experience. Concretized experience
is oftentimes removed from reality as well. In some instances,
visual pictures remain, but affective states are nonexistent; or if
the affective (phobic) state remains, there are no visual memories. The attempt to recall the visual picture or the affective
experience through hypnotic suggestion is possible, but to recall
the terror along with the actual experience seems impossible
because most likely it is nonexistent. The person's sense of self
was annihilated by the trauma. In most traumatic situations the
visual picture remains intact without feelings of terror, or the
terror remains without the concrete experiences. Physical

sensations of pain or of a smell may be the only memories that exist in very serious cases of abuse (Blume, 1989; Frederickson, 1992; Perlman, 1993).

Forgotten memories rooted in deep despair and psychic annihilation are profound determinants of the self. Because they are forgotten, they are insidious signposts on unconscious roads in the mind that the victim understandably tries to avoid at all costs. To get on that road back to terror is devastating, but to avoid facing one's terror means to take the road to self-destruction. This is the most difficult crossroad in the life of a victim—to reexperience the terror of psychic annihilation or to live a life in avoidance and self-destruction. I believe that many people find themselves at this crossroad between avoidance and denial or terror, whether or not they can articulate the experience. I believe that society and social norms encourage the individual to deny or avoid his or her inner experiences, which leads the individual to be self-destructive. Acceptance of inner experiences of terror is something that people are encouraged to forget about by using drugs, alcohol, and other forms of self-annihilating, escapist behavior. It is not only that one's inner life is not embraced but that it is actually ignored by contemporary materialistic visions of the meaning of life.

*   *   *

Being at the emotional crossroad, between the familiar road of avoidance of painful experiences through self-destructiveness and self-hatred and the unfamiliar road that takes you back to those traumatic, terror-filled experiences, is an extremely hazardous and difficult fork in the road. Most people who have been emotionally, sexually, or physically abused by their caregivers have consciously or unconsciously gotten to this place on the map of their psychic life. I know I have been at this crossroad many times. The more familiar path for me was hating myself and feeling defective. It was an organizing experience to feel bad about myself because it was so familiar. Taking the unfamiliar path back to the terror of abuse and rage was psycholog-ically impossible to do alone. The unknown was extremely scary, so I have worked very hard to stay on this road of the subjective reality of my own feelings. Dr. Ace has walked beside me down this road. It has been difficult because I have limited visual pictures and few concrete memories that explain to me what happened and why I was so bad.

Yet I have my emotional memories and a guide, Dr. Ace, to find the path to my past and forgotten history. My emotional memories are primarily of emotional annihilation or extreme emotional isolation and terror. Concrete visual pictures of trau-matic events are gone, except for several specific memories, pho-bias, and symptoms of forgetting. With the sense of safety that Dr. Ace's attunement provides me, I can now tolerate the emo-tional terror of my childhood memories.

*   *   *

In my first analysis I was still on that avoidance road to self-destruction. I tried to convince myself that being the best I could be was a way to deal with feeling bad about myself. Dr. Z encouraged me to take this path to hell. Success didn't deal with the problem, however. I was still taking a detour because I didn't really like myself. I had no idea why I was bad. I knew Dr. Z's interpretation: I was the bad twin while my sister was the good twin. I knew that this was true for other twins, for I had written a book about personality development in twins. Nonetheless, this understanding didn't help me feel entitled to my feelings. Dr. Z's interpretation was initially insightful, but later it was a source of intense frustration. I knew I had a distorted self-perception. I believed I had to reestablish a good sense of myself through accomplishments. I did feel good about my achieve-ments, but only when I was achieving. Otherwise, I easily forgot about my achievements. They were not integrated into my psychic structure, as Dr. Ace pointed out to me when I began my second analysis (Kohut, 1977, 1984; Stolorow & Atwood,

1987). I knew in my head who I was, but emotionally I would forget. I lacked a psychic structure or a container to accept myself because I had never dealt with the reason why I was bad in the eyes of my family. I needed to know more.

The emotional reality of getting beyond feeling bad about myself has been the most difficult and exciting challenge of my life. For me to accept my feelings as real has taken a great deal of courage and an analytic experience that fosters trust.

I understand that my difficulty with feeling entitled to my feelings stems from a basic issue related to traumatic child abuse; namely, the child who is abused cannot tolerate the belief that their caregivers *do not* value them for themselves. The experience of being an object for the caregiver's satisfaction is emotionally unbearable. The defensive reaction is to not feel entitled to care or attention. In other words, it is emotionally easier to feel unworthy yourself than to accept that the other person views you as worthless. Further, when you are so extremely vulnerable to the cruelty of others, there is a confusion that sets in from terror. It is like a cognitive dissonance. The mind and soul cannot tolerate the terror unless it is justified or sanctioned by the other. Once the individual's sense of self has been compromised in such a way, it is very difficult to maintain a consistent sense of self-worth because mini flashbacks and traumatic terror easily undermine the confident sense of self. The trauma must be acknowledged by the analyst and understood if the victim is to become a confident survivor. Perlman (1993) writes:

> After a time, visual and auditory memories begin emerging. Next, the patient experiences shock and disbelief, saying, "I must be crazy, this can't be true; my parents were not like this; how could this be?" The patient may wish to believe that he or she is crazy, or making these images up, rather than believing them with all the implications of their veracity. At these moments, the patient usually turns to the analyst, and demands that the analyst tell him or her if these images are true. At this moment, the experience may shift to a flashback, and the patient may actually experience being "back there" in the memory. Feelings of disgust and being

bad alternate with disbelief, and the patient may make statements like, "I must be bad, I must have caused it. I must be crazy." If, at any time in this process, the therapist/analyst is not supportive or understanding, or if he or she in any way interferes, the memories will go back underground into the body. The patient is then very willing to go back into denial. If the therapist is empathically connected with the patient, then the work can begin to fit together the pieces of the patient's childhood. Next, the patient tends to mourn the loss of the childhood fantasy of well-being, and of having good parents (pp. 9–10).

Intermittent psychological annihilation was what I was subjected to as a young child by my father and my brother. I know that I am not alone in having lived through this type of childhood, for I have worked with many patients who have similar symptoms of amnesia, phobias, panic attacks, and an overdetermined need for achievement. Far too many individuals lose their sense of entitlement and sense of self-worth, which is crucial to their self-development, because of cruel and traumatic events brought about by others who are supposedly their caregivers. Clinicians view these patients as suffering from mental disorders, when in actuality they are suffering from the terror of painful experiences. Children and adults who have been terrorized by their caregivers need compassion and understanding. Unfortunately, far too often clinicians give them a diagnosis or an evaluation of their mental deficits. This is when diagnosis becomes a criminal act perpetrated on victims of traumatic childhood abuse by the helping professionals. Labeling an individual's pain diminishes the reality of his or her past and creates further misunderstanding and narcissistic injury.

* * *

After all my writing and all my thought and inner reflection, I am still ashamed that I experienced and suffered from childhood abuse. I was mistreated so severely that I cannot even remember in detail what happened to me. Yet one important change is that I can now understand that it was not my fault, and I can now quickly come to an intellectual understanding of what I am entitled to from others, although feeling emotionally entitled is far more difficult for me. I still devalue my own feelings and lose my sense of entitlement when I am totally overwhelmed and stressed out by life situations.

I often wonder whether I would have been able to recall more details of the specific forms of abuse had my first analysis dealt with the problems caused by incest. Perhaps then the shame associated with my amnesia would have been diffused. This is a question for which I can never have an answer. I regret that I have lived so long without understanding why I felt so bad about myself.

I don't believe in hypnosis, although Dr. Ace has described this as a possibility with me. I feel that the experience of being in the control of another, without any recourse, would be too difficult for me. I still fear the consequences of knowing something I cannot remember on my own. I don't know if my feelings about hypnosis will change. I don't even believe that knowing is the answer. There are no answers—just understanding and acceptance.

I am not convinced that confronting my brother and getting the whole truth is possible. My father and mother are dead. Although my mother remembered enough to convince me that I am correct about being abused sexually, I also believe in the subjective truth of my own feelings. I know enough about sexual abuse from working with patients and studying the literature in the field to accept that some perpetrators can never admit to their misdeeds. This I have also learned from my own experiences with my father and brother.

I often hear this reality of abject denial from my patients. For example, recently the young woman Lori, to whom I felt so immediately connected in the beginning of our work, was able to confront her mother about her experiences of being sexually abused by her father. Her mother was at first horrified; then she explained to my patient, Lori, that the babysitter had sexually abused her. Lori's mother listened to her feelings about her memories of her father's sexual abuse. Even though she was initially horrified, she would not or could not accept her daughter's memories of these traumatic experiences as real. Lori's mother called Lori back and left a message on her answering machine calling her a liar. Lori's father then wrote her a letter denying any kind of abusive behavior. As might be expected, my patient became understandably confused. She called to ask me if I thought that she was making her feelings up, as her mother had accused her of doing. Had it really happened? I reassured her that she had been abused emotionally and sexually. She began to talk with me about her feelings of unreality and how she had lost contact with her sense of self and of being sexually abused. She could remember only the emotional abuse of her father's anger. She talked to me of her fears that her father would come to her home and hurt her, and it was then that she called a detective service. This act of self-protection allowed her to reconnect with her sense of self and her memories of how her father had molested her many, many times in her childhood.

There was never any confirmation or affirmation from my patient's family about the traumatic experiences she was forced to endure because of her father's out-of-control, alcoholic, perverse behavior and her mother's inability to protect Lori from her father.

Her mother writes apologetically but ambivalently, speaking with love, sadness, anger and denial:

Dear Lori,

I have thought of you so often since we spoke on the phone. I'm so sorry, Lori, that I didn't know something so terrible has happened to you or at least you think it has. Could it just be a terrible nightmare? For years I have had a nightmare about the war and I wake up crying and afraid, but my dream didn't happen to me. Your father and I will do everything we can to make you realize that he never could have done such a thing. I am so glad you told me. What if your father had died or both of us and you were left for the rest of your life believing this. By now you will have received a copy of the letter he sent to Elaine [Elaine is Lori's ex-sister-in-law].

Love,

Mother

The following is a letter written to Elaine, a copy of which was sent to my patient from her father:

Dear Elaine,

I am writing this letter to ask for your assistance in dealing with a serious problem concerning Lori.

As you may be aware, Lori has been seeing a psychiatrist for counseling and therapy since well before she and Joe broke up. More recently, she has become convinced that her emotional problems stem from having been sexually molested as a child. She has confided to Joy that this notion was first suggested to her by Joe, who, she claims, accused me of having molested her. At that time, her reaction was to vigorously deny the suggestion. Indeed, up until the time when Joe made this unfounded allegation, she apparently had no recollection of any such traumatic experience during her childhood. Unfortunately, during the period since, she has grown to harbor doubts and become convinced that such an incident did take place. She now firmly believes that she was molested when she was about eleven years old by someone big who held her down and later terrified her into keeping silent. More recently, she has come to believe the suggestion she attributes to Joe, that I am the individual responsible.

You can perhaps imagine how Joy and I feel in the face of this pernicious accusation, which is totally untrue and completely unsubstantiated. I have reported the incident to my authorities because of the potential implications to my security clearance. In addition, since I have nothing to hide, I have offered to take a polygraph or any other test administered by an appropriate authority to prove my innocence. I categorically deny that I was ever involved in any sexual activity involving my daughter or any other minor. I find the thought of such an act abhorrent and believe anybody making such a false accusation is badly in need of help.

Neither Joy nor I have any recollection of any behavior by Lori to suggest that such an incident took place during her childhood. Although there is the possibility that a child of her age at the time could have completely masked her reaction to such a traumatic incident, I find the notion farfetched. I also challenge the suggestion that she was ever terrified of me. I believe defiant would be a more apt description of her attitude on those occasions where we had serious differences of opinion.

Sincerely,

Henry
[Lori's father]

* * *

The reactions of Lori's parents, although horrifyingly typical of the denial characteristic of sexually abusive families, were extremely painful for my patient to bear. Understandably, they were experienced as a revictimization of earlier experiences. My patient has chosen not to speak with her father or mother until they both acknowledge that she was molested by her father over a period of at least eight years.

I had a similar experience with my twin sister when she read the first draft of this manuscript. She was horrified that the story would be out in the open for everyone to read. At first my pain was definitely less important to her than the shame of the truth and keeping up a good family image. She could understand my pain in private, but then she became, as I had been at first, obsessed with the truth and the details. At first she didn't want to believe what I was saying. She seemed to be more upset for herself than for me. But gradually as I stood firm behind my beliefs and feelings, she began to listen to what I had to say. It was painful for her because she felt ashamed and guilty, because it didn't happen to her, and because she didn't protect me from being hurt. It was our mother's strength and my husband's support that finally helped my sister to tolerate her feelings about my incestuous experiences.

* * *

I believe there is hope for understanding the issue of sexual abuse beyond what clinicians presently understand. I believe that this will happen when parents, mental health professionals, and victims themselves become more open and honest about the potential for incest and the events surrounding this shameful and humiliating experience. Although my shame still exists, I believe it is far less intense than it was before I was able to talk about it openly. I believe that other mental health professionals and patients can also become more open to the possibility of sexual abuse and explore it more seriously as a possibility for emotional symptoms.

Clearly, there are long-lasting and serious aftereffects of incest that are amenable to intensive psychotherapeutic interventions. Developing trust in the analyst and his or her understanding and belief in your subjective experience is crucial. If the analyst can accept that the abuse occurred and stay with the patient's feelings, then there is hope for recovery. But often the issue of sexual abuse is covered up by shame and disbelief, creating more of a mystery than it needs to be. Clinicians can blame Freud for originally covering up this knowledge, as discussed in Masson's (1991) book *Final Analysis*. "Passing the buck" is not as effective as the clinician's taking responsibility for understanding what has transpired with his or her own patients.

* * *

For me, forgotten memories and forgotten feelings are symptoms of traumatic child abuse. My true self and my compensatory false self became confused to cover up painful feelings of shame and humiliation that were related to sexual abuse. The cost to my development of an authentic self was enormous. I was out of balance because of the secret. As a consequence, I became isolated and withdrawn. My intellectual strengths were overdetermined, overcompensating to keep unbearable feelings of terror, rage, and hopelessness away.

Other symptoms have surfaced besides gaps in a continuous sense of self and have created serious depression. Specifically, I became overly concerned with the reactions of others. I wanted to please everyone and keep everyone happy to avoid getting in trouble and in this way avoid being abused again. This pattern of concern for the care and welfare of others became pervasive and self-destructive. I learned to be compliant as well as more concerned about others than myself. I learned to put my feelings aside or to use my feelings to support others. I did not have a clue about how to take care of myself without concerning myself with others. I was selfless and overidentified with other people because I didn't know how to take my feelings seriously and follow them. My feelings were hidden behind secret walls. I gave up my feelings to depression, withdrawal, disavowal, and denial.

I also gave up my feelings to inhibitions. I withdrew instead of being confrontive. I was always smoothing things out and covering up the truth of my feelings and experiences. I could more easily say to myself, "You are strange," than to accept my sense of the other person's limitations. The sad truth is that I was led to believe this was the road to my salvation by my father, my brother, and Dr. Z. Actually, it was the road to a crippling depression.

I believe that I am not alone in my despair. Other women have been grossly misled by their caregivers and then their analysts or therapists. The problems created by psychic annihilation, as a result of traumatic childhood abuse, are insidious and pervasive. For me, the underlying issue is that people ask for help and are exploited because they are vulnerable. This is the very serious dilemma that the victim faces on the road to becoming a survivor.

EIGHT

Knots of Shame

Shame

Shame is a feeling:
of intense pain
of worthlessness
of feeling defective
of being nothing
of no hope
of no one caring
of isolation
of oblivion
of pain in my pelvis
of nausea
of being stuck on the edge of a cliff with no help
of being disfigured
of being naked and scared.

I was hiding from my shame, and I knew it. I was tied up in knots of shame, and I knew it. I had one foot in the tarpits of shame, one foot on the ground, and one arm tied to my support squadron, which included my analyst, my husband, my children, my mother, and my sister. If I was going to be a survivor, I knew I needed help pulling myself out of my intense feelings of self-hatred. I knew that my sense of defectiveness was real and that it was tearing me apart. I knew that my frightening childhood experiences were real. I had gone beyond and through my denial. As enraged as I was, I was more ashamed. I felt so damaged. At first it seemed that I spoke in a whisper about what had happened to me. I let innuendos about my shame emerge in conversations as I continued to write about my feelings and experiences as a secret survivor.

I was relieved that I was finally sure about why I felt so bad about myself. Mine was a classic case out of a textbook on childhood sexual abuse; I was bad because I was seduced into being traumatically sexually overstimulated and abused. I was bad because I allowed my father and brother to control me. Their logic was self-serving and illogical. I knew this as an adult. I was finally able to hold onto my rage at my father and my brother and not think I was making it up. It was their fault. They had sexually abused me and emotionally victimized me. But why was I still so ashamed? I felt so damaged, not only because I had symptoms that I could not hide but because I had been victimized by my father and brother. To make my pain worse and more confusing, part of the trauma had been reenacted in my first analysis.

When I think back on related feeling states of being damaged, it is not only intensely painful but also confusing and alienating. I now understand why I could not talk about my shame and why I felt so humiliated and isolated. I did not want anyone to know that I was so damaged. I wanted to isolate myself from the world. I can think back on my states of depressions and the sense of shame I had before I recovered memories of the trauma when I had wanted to lock myself up in my closet rather than face the world. I can remember how many times I wished I were dead I remember, even as a young child and far into late adolescence, running away from my parents' house and my mother and sister trying to find me. Concerned, they were always confused by my running away. I know now this action was related to my early sense that I was damaged and that the only place for me to be was in the closet, hidden away, living on a secluded island, or dead. At my worst and most desperate moments, my shame about being damaged led to terrible and pervasive feelings of worthlessness that I could not share with anyone. I wanted to hide my feelings from the world. I was successful in keeping my secret from everyone, including my conscious self.

Then I met Dr. Ace.

* * *

These events and feeling states sound so tragic as I write about them. Fortunately, my sense of being damaged is now less painful because there is a happy ending that comes from knowing the truth. Most of my sadness is in the past, and I feel entitled to my place on earth. I feel valuable and important to many people, but feeling valuable and believing in myself came slowly from my second analytic experience, which allowed me first to make contact with my forgotten memories and then to connect with people who I trusted might be interested in my traumatic experiences from childhood.

The events that led me to begin speaking up outside of my second analytic experience are somewhat out of sequence in my mind. I began writing *Forgotten Memories*. I showed my writing to others. I had to speak to others as a reaction to what I wrote. It was difficult, not only because I felt vulnerable but because it was painful. My preference was not to expose my damaged self. People had distinct reactions to my manuscript—"good" to "bad," "horrified" to "crucial." It was difficult to listen to what others had to say about what I had written and still believe they valued me. I was still keeping my past at arm's length and denying the abuse or getting too close to the past and feeling incapacitated, like a helpless child.

There is, for the incest victim, so much shame and such a sense of being defective that even if you know the truth—that you were traumatically hurt, that it's not your fault, and that you're not bad—you still feel damaged, defective, and ashamed.

Oftentimes I felt it was impossible to stop feeling ashamed. The first and most familiar way that I dealt with my sense of shame and damage was to try to cover it up. I became a successful and highly competent professional. However, I was also alone with a secret that only a selected group of people knew about. I was worried that people would glare at me if they knew who I really was or what had happened to me. I was also worried that other people would be overly concerned or too polite. It was hard to trust that other people would understand, even though I knew better. I knew the statistics indicate that up to one in three children is sexually exploited. I spoke with patients who were themselves survivors. I read all the books about survivors of incest. Nonetheless it remained difficult for me to believe that people wouldn't think, "It was your fault. You were a bad little girl." Yet it was more than that as well. Incest is a taboo in our society, so that just admitting to being a victim made me feel even more alone and damaged. But I knew I needed to talk with others about who I was in order to diffuse my sense that I was permanently scarred psychologically by my childhood.

*   *   *

My first speaking-up event was a total disaster. I was encouraged by close colleagues and my husband to apply to a new, supposedly free-thinking psychoanalytic institute in our community. My friends and my husband respected my work and wanted me to join their institute. I was skeptical, but I was also very flattered; so I decided to apply. I turned in the questionnaire and completed the interviews. I was stunned by the feedback I received indirectly—that I wasn't "okay enough" to be admitted to the new institute. Somehow, the admissions committee couldn't believe that my early traumatic experiences and my ensuing rage at my first analyst were acceptable or normal. Somehow I was at fault in their eyes for being enraged at my analyst. They implied that I had not been able to take in and accept what Dr. Z had to offer to me. Within the psychoanalytic institute, the trauma of my childhood was uncannily reenacted. The perpetrators, the admissions committee, were innocent; I was the bad one again. It was my fault that Dr. Z had missed the seriousness of my sense of worthlessness and that I was so angry about my sense of betrayal. They implied that my anger made me an unstable personality. Besides offering their opinion about how I might function, they made me feel damaged. The admissions committee at the new institute reminded me of the old pain and depression I had felt when I was treated as if I were defective, both in childhood and in my analysis. Dr. Ace encouraged me to withdraw my application before it got to the final committee, so I did. I was relieved because I couldn't take the pain of feeling damaged again. I felt hurt, but this time I knew that they were wrong. I knew that I needed to take my story to someone who would listen and not feel so personally affronted. They did not want to understand me. In the end, the club members always see themselves as right. Some things never change, even in "new" groups.

I guess that I could have gotten stuck on this experience with the new psychoanalytic institute, which made me feel unacceptable because of my past traumas; but my situation didn't permit me the time to ruminate about these painful events. The day that classes began at the new institute, my mother was diagnosed as having inoperable, terminal cancer. At most she had three to six months to live. I was so concerned and consumed with my unexpected loss that I put aside my feelings about my experiences with the new psychoanalytic institute.

I took over charge of my mother's care. Thankfully, my sister was helpful and trusted my decisions, as did my mother. My brother was impossible to communicate with and emotionally unavailable, as he had always been. My husband and children were extremely helpful and available, as were my aunts and uncles. It was a difficult six months. I did a lot of talking with my twin sister, who became, as she says, "my loyal servant." Of course, she is too opinionated and outspoken to be a servant. But she was finally able to talk with me about our relationship with our brother and the legacy in our family. Although we were 45 years old before we agreed about our past, our reconnecting was important in my recovery. My sister was finally able to get beyond her fear and gave up her allegiance to our brother and the family myth that we were a normal family. She now saw me as the family victim. She wanted to share in my shame. She wanted to help me to remember what I had forgotten. I felt as if she were no longer ashamed of me and, in turn, ashamed of our twinship. She could tolerate her own discomfort with the *truth*, although it was seriously disturbing to her. My sister wrote down her thoughts about my incestuous experiences for me:

April 29, 1992

Dear Barbara,

Why could I not accept my discomfort? Was it too hard to accept my shame? Of course it was hard to accept my shame. Whether it was the shame of the incest or just the shame I felt that goes along with being a twin, which made me feel like I did not have control over my life.

I guess I had enough of seeing you suffer. I simply decided to live in the here and now and take your side, since I was already on your side. I guess I decided to stop fighting with myself and accept our twinship.

For many years, all those years when you were in analysis, I felt like I didn't know as much as you did, so I couldn't make a good decision. I felt intimidated by the fact that both you and your husband were professionals in the field of psychology and psychiatry. Thank God I went beyond that and just decided to be your twin sister. I accepted my shame, the shame I feel as a twin because it is so hard for me to be a twin, to be part of you as well as my own self, you who can face your secrets and fight for what you want. Accepting you in a way is accepting my cowardice, and I was a coward and I was afraid.

Finally, I could listen to what had happened to you and not feel as intensely involved in it as you were. So I could objectify your pain, which had always been my pain. Then we could work together to get beyond the feelings of shame, the feelings of self-hatred, double self-hatred for who I was as an individual and for who I was as your twin sister.

It was quite simple separating myself from our problem when I realized that it was a different problem for each of us. It only took me 45 years to realize that it was so simple. We each had different problems. . . .

I have stopped being in the middle and trying to pretend that our childhood is too complex to understand. I accepted that I have to see life for what it is, to see our childhood for what it was. I am dealing with my shame.

It isn't so hard; secrets are stressful, secrets take time, secrets lock you up inside and imprison you in a fear of your own. Having a second family, a brother-in-law, a nephew, a niece, and two big dogs is a great joy, a gift I finally allowed myself. . . .

You were always and still are my big sister, and that is finally okay. In fact it is a great comfort; as a cohort I am not so bad myself; I can stir up lots of trouble, like you have and believe me I will—I have lots of years to make up for.

Love,

Marjorie

* * *

Although she was very ill, my mother was able to speak with me about my feelings of being sexually abused. She believed me. She was concerned about helping me. She finally admitted that she had also been a victim of my brother's arrogance and distrust, as well as my father's emotional and physical abuse. I realized to what extent she had suffered her entire life. For those last six months, my sister, my mother, and I talked openly about our past. This was extremely helpful because it cleansed my mind and helped me vent my anger. My mother was a smart woman. She had tried her best and was truly sorry not to have been able to protect me from my father and brother. She could admit that to me. She didn't want any more secrets before she died. I had the sense that she knew what she had accomplished with her life and that I loved her in spite of what we had suffered through. She told me that I would survive, as did other women who had been molested. She hoped I could make the world a better place to live and gave me courage to try. My mother knew I would publish this book because she believed I could help other people understand their emotional pain. She was proud of me for speaking up.

*   *   *

By the time my mother died, I had spoken to close relatives about being sexually abused. They were accepting, concerned, and hopeful that I would put my past behind me. They made me feel that I was okay, no matter what had happened. Their supportiveness made me feel less damaged and less ashamed.

Even though I had asked my mother and sister not to talk to my brother, they explained to me that they had spoken to him about my manuscript and my feelings because of their concern for me. My brother's reaction was to say that I was just over-reacting to some "dirty things" that he had done. He never directly denied to me that he had used me as a sex object. His reaction showed that he was the same arrogant person he had always been. He was never able to take responsibility for trau-matizing me. Nevertheless, our turbulent and hateful interac-tions were frozen. He would not speak to me, and I would not speak to him. Even at my mother's funeral we did not speak. My brother's common-law wife stared at me and tried to make me feel "crazy" with her hostile smile. After the funeral, every-one except the rabbi knew why I was so angry with my brother. No one said, "Try to forgive him." He has never spoken with me about what happened with us as children. No one who knows the story has suggested that we try to get along. I know that some victim-survivors want to make peace with their abu-sers, but I don't have any interest in reconciliation.

I have spoken with attorneys about suing my brother for my years of psychoanalytic treatment. All I spoke with seemed to think I would not win the case because I have never been hospitalized and all my treatment has been completed in an analyst's office. In their estimation I am too high functioning to win, for I have been married for 25 years and have raised two well-adjusted children. And although Dr. Ace said he would testify on my behalf, my case is not a good one, according to the attorneys. They are so uninformed about the trauma of incest! Even though I want my brother to pay a share of my therapy bills, I do not want to have to educate an attorney to get him to do so. This would be a thankless and futile task for me.

* * *

Several themes are becoming clearer in my own personal history, which I think are common phenomena that all survivors of sexual abuse encounter. It is important to accentuate these themes, for it is a long and difficult road that a survivor travels on until he or she gets to a place where the shame and sense of being damaged diminish. The first step is for survivors to recognize that they have been abused. This can take a very long time. Then survivors need help from others who encourage understanding, acceptance, and tolerance of the traumatic events. Basic support from a therapist is essential, but support from others is also critical. Oftentimes an external crisis will lead survivors to seek help and to open up to others who can make them feel protected and safe. This kind of protection from feeling ashamed was most important to me and to those I have worked with who have been able to recover from traumatic sexual abuse.

It doesn't always *happen* that incest survivors remember, let alone seek help, even if they have the right kind of support and protection. I am one of the fortunate ones in having had both professional help and personal support.

Dealing with my shame, I believe, was the turning point to recovery for me. First, I had to get through the depression created by my rage and understand what had happened to me, and who I was, before I could deal with my shame. As my depression gradually faded away with help and hope, like fog lifting off the beach, I could more clearly see what had happened to me. What a relief that I was more positive and less obsessed with the meaningless of my life than I had been when I first consulted Dr. Ace over four years ago! The task for me, with the assistance of Dr. Ace and my support squadron, was to accept that what I had experienced didn't make me "damaged goods." I finally integrated emotionally my intellectual sense of my childhood when I realized that all my denial and forgetting was a defense against remembering what had really happened. I came to the point where the denial no longer worked for me. Reality, as painful as it is to accept, is "where I am at."

Gradually I began to give up my obsession with remembering and describing the details of my incestuous experiences. I remember saying to Dr. Ace that I knew enough now. I finally said, "I don't want to remember any more." Eventually, as Dr. Ace had predicted, I began to recover more memories of my past.

My husband and I took a ski trip to Yosemite, a place out of my childhood. That first night I dreamed that a man was in bed with me, masturbating himself and fondling me. I woke up and saw that it had been a dream. My husband was asleep beside me. Not only had the memory become clearer, but the related feeling states were also clearer. I felt so panicked, so agitated. My husband and I talked about my dream and my feelings of insecurity and rising panic. He tried to reassure me that I was totally safe, that there were no intruders. My problem, for the day, was not in our control. The snow had melted, and we couldn't go cross-country skiing. Ever practical, my husband suggested that we take a hike, which might make me feel more relaxed. We climbed Vernal Falls and Nevada Falls, a hike that we have done together many times. But this time, I was terrified by the cliffs and the icy steps. I was sure I was going to die. I was totally agoraphobic. The day seemed too bright, and I couldn't calm down, no matter how many miles we hiked. The next evening I had a similar dream about the same person in bed with me. The dream recreated a memory that I had; it was terrifyingly real. The next morning we went home. I had had enough of my memories of what had happened to me as a child. Dr. Ace remained calm when I talked with him. I, on the other hand, felt terrified. My sister wanted to hear about my dreams in detail. My mother, who was dying, was just happy that I was safe at home and alive.

The terror created by these two dreams that spilled into my waking life seemed to be totally different from the exhaustion or fog of my long-standing depression or the emptiness and loneliness of the amnesia. The terror was bright, like a bright light on a sandy shore on a hot summer day. The terror was truly frightening. I felt so insignificant, so vulnerable and at risk. Calming myself down took time. I had no problem deciding that I didn't want to go back to that state of mind again.

Accepting my feelings of shame and talking about them with Dr. Ace and then with my family unquestionably led to the two dreams of my brother masturbating and fondling me. Memories, the dreams, along with the associated feeling state of terror were necessary to alleviate some of the intense shame I harbored.

I feel now that I may recover more memories and that the terror may return. I fear these deeply hidden memories and the feelings that have made me feel damaged and ashamed. But my fears are not so far-reaching as they used to be because I feel safe and protected. I know people will believe me.

I feel that I can protect myself from my fear because it came from traumatic childhood experiences. I feel more alive because I can now write about my different states of mind—the depression, amnesia, shame, and terror—as well as forgotten memories, which are a reaction to traumatization.

* * *

My mother died shortly after the trip to Yosemite. I felt totally sad and alone. Yet I had an excellent analyst who had cured me. My family remained energetic and supportive, and meanwhile I maintained an entire private practice. In addition, at last I had my twin sister's support. The sadness and loneliness, I believe, derived from an internal identification with my mother, who herself had been a victim of all kinds of abuse during her life. The pain of missing my mother remains profound. My mother had been my secret sister. She understood my pain because she had also experienced the shame and humiliation that comes from being victimized, although we never had time to discuss how she felt about being a victim.

After her death, my mother's shame no longer fueled me or kept me from taking the time to express myself. My mother's wish that there be no more secrets helped me begin writing again. I still feel ashamed of myself occasionally, when others are unhappy or disappointed in me, but this state of mind is infrequent and less intense than it used to be. I feel more loved, more understood, and less vulnerable to feeling ashamed.

My shame has lost some of its intense power to make me feel bad and damaged. The recovered memories of my pain are alive and organized. Now I use my memories to help other people I work with, write for, or talk to understand their shame and the sense of damage and pain it causes.

NINE

My Secret Sisters

The family myth that I was the bad twin and my sister was the good twin survived because it successfully masked the truth that I had been molested by my father and brother. The painful, sad irony is that this mythical system, psychologically enforced, was destructive to me, my sister, and my mother. At the age of 41, when I realized I was bad because I had been molested, the truth was unmasked. And the truth—that I had been sexually abused—had created and then bolstered the split between my mother, my sister, and me. The intolerable torn relationships with my mother and my sister, which I ambivalently held onto after getting married, began to mend. As a result there came new meaning, new life, into my relations first with my mother and then my sister.

It is difficult to believe, but not impossible to accept, that who we were was chipped out of the family's corrupt mythology. It was, after all, the "enemy"—that out-of-control part of my father and brother—that survived, enforcing the myth that I was bad and deserved whatever I got, and that my sister was good and never ever made mistakes. The same family myth perpetuated the belief that my extremely smart mother was incompetent and guilty for whatever went wrong—which was always everything. This was my psychological identification with my mother. Fortunately, I was more able to act on my own than was my mother and less afraid of, or less in reverence of, my father and brother.

Nevertheless, this malignant assumption, rooted deeply in the family's collective psychic, trapped and poisoned us in a soil that could never sustain life. It was that evil in our roots that poisoned my mother and led to her early death. In the end of her life she could neither eat nor breathe. I believe that it was my father and brother's self-indulgence, selfishness, corruption, and abuse that kept her from taking what she needed from life. I always wanted to help my mother compensate for her past experiences as a victim because I identified with her. She was my secret sister. Unconsciously, I wanted my mother to be a survivor; she, in turn, wanted the same for me.

*   *   *

I never consciously remembered how seriously my mother had been traumatized and abused until three months before her death from endometrial cancer with metastases. My amnesia kept me from remembering not only my emotional pain but also her pain. And although my sister didn't forget the chaos and abuse of our childhood, we had never taken the time to discuss the abuse in our past because between the ages of 21 and 45 my sister and I had lived very separate lives, for the most part due to my experiences with my first analyst. My mother had been too ashamed of her physical and psychological pain to speak out about it to me. She was strong enough to keep her physical pain to herself—the beatings she continually received from my father and then the pain from the cancer. Her psychological pain from lifelong abuse and disappointments, which she withdrew into, overwhelmed her and ultimately killed her. She never wanted to die. Had she been able to talk about her own shame and sadness, perhaps she might still be here to read my words, to share my pain and sadness, and to take joy in my relief and triumph in coming to understand the incest.

* * *

I remember the morning the surgeons told us that my mother had terminal cancer. *It was a shock.* Just an hour before the doctors operated, my mother had said, "I never thought this would happen to me, dear." Perhaps she knew something the doctors hadn't known before the surgery.

I will never forget how teary-eyed the kind doctors who operated on her looked when they told us that she had only three to six months to live, with no hope for remission. They must have sensed that we loved her so very much and that she loved us, and that her life was still important. But as sure as they were of their predictions, the doctors were wrong. Miraculously, the cancer went into remission. My mother lived to fight the cancer, but she could not fight her psychological pain, which was too malignant and deeply rooted in her childhood.

I remember carefully choosing the finest and most respectable oncologist for my mother. With much concern I told him that right before my father died, she had had a nervous breakdown in which she had totally withdrawn from the world. I explained how worried I was that she would once again become depressed and withdrawn. I knew that she was emotionally fragile and feared death. The oncologist, who was well experienced, told me frankly, "She will never live long enough to get depressed again." He was wrong, too.

Three months after my mother's surgery, she became paralyzed physically and emotionally by an overwhelming depression, even though the cancer was in remission. The oncologist finally recommended his brother, a psychiatrist experienced in working with cancer patients, for a consultation. My mother agreed to see this psychiatrist because my husband and I insisted that it would help her. She trusted us and attended this meeting, although still extremely frail.

I will never forget that one session with me, my mother, my husband, and Elena, her constant caregiver and friend. The psychiatrist wanted her to explain to him why she was so angry.

He wanted to know if the depression was organic (if the cancer had spread to her brain) or if it had a history rooted in her past. My mother spoke about her relationship with my father. Her words recalled in me feelings of terror repressed for at least 30 years. It was eerie to hear my mother talk about how terribly she had been abused by my father. I knew by listening to her that she would never have put up with his terrorizing her had she not herself been seriously hurt as a child. Recognizing how deep-seated her pain was, I realized that my father and my brother had only perpetuated what someone else had started. She had never really known how to protect herself from other people's abuse. I know that even though she was strong, brave, kind, and smart, she could never have protected me from the demons that had irreparably hurt her.

*   *   *

The experience of listening to my mother speak about her emotional pain was intensely sad as well as enraging. The past and the present were alive in her words, there for me to remember always. There was a part of my past that came alive in a way that my present could never erase or forget.

Because of my mother's experiences as a victim, she could understand me in a way that has been inaccessible to others. Despite my being surrounded by the love and empathy from family, friends, and colleagues, I deeply miss her understanding and her concern.

*   *   *

Now that my mother is no longer alive to share with me her concerns about my well-being, my twin sister has become my new ally in fighting my shame. She helps me remember by reminding me of facts I have forgotten. In response to my request that she write to me about our childhood, she has shared the following thoughts, which serve to reaffirm the incest in my past and why I have "forgotten memories." I am exceptionally fortunate to have a living memory bank donor to share the subjective memories of our past.

August 5, 1992

Dear Barbara,

On reading your manuscript, *Forgotten Memories*, which is about your childhood and mine too, I realize that I recall memories that until now I have taken for granted that we shared. These memories, some of them only images, seem perfectly characteristic of our early childhood life and for that reason it is remarkable, astonishing in a way that may take time to really understand. I can't imagine why you don't have these memories.

I always felt you had been hurt, but never knew why or even why I felt that it was something about you, some desperation and some sadness that I knew I didn't have. I always wanted to help you but I was too close to it and knew that I had to live my own life—I know I believed you could survive, but that we would take different paths away from home; I am glad we are coming back together now that we both have our own families and professions.

I know that you were treated as the bad twin, but I suffered as well. From Alan's arrogance, nurtured by mother, I developed my low sense of self-esteem; I really believed that I was stupid because Alan was so stingy with his approval and because his approval was so important through mother via him to me. Thus the rift between mother and Alan at her death seems even more painful for me, but mostly for mother and for Alan. Why couldn't they just communicate with each other? I have had to learn to believe in myself; even with my successes I devalue my strengths and expect approval when most people are just pleased with my capability and don't think about my need for approval. But Alan was always supposed to approve of me and he was and always has been so stingy in his approval.

now on to my memories . . .

I remember mother always criticizing father for his ham radio. I remember that he once gave mother a black eye after an argument. I remember that she lied and said she had slipped in the bathtub. But I knew daddy had hit her.

I remember her being afraid that daddy would run away from her or that he would get drunk. I remember father having a terrible temper and my being afraid of his temper.

I don't really have any explicit sexual memories—I think about mother being afraid of daddy being drunk, which somehow relates to sexuality—perhaps being out of control—mother hating father to be out of control and father hating mother for always trying to control him and Alan trying to keep people calm.

I remember playing footsie with you and Alan torturing you and my going along with the game because you were more like mother, more like the victim of the family—and I know it sounds sick but it was your role, being the victim and the mother like mother—I was afraid to become a mother because being a mother was something I was afraid of from the way you and mother were treated in the family.

I also remember that you couldn't sleep when the TV was on too loud.

I remember one night being terrified by the Dr. Jekyll and Mr. Hyde movie.

I remember our bedroom with the Raggedy Ann and Andy wallpaper and I remember being afraid of images in the wallpaper.

I remember being afraid of fish like you are; I remember being terrified of having to go fishing at Girl Scout camp at Catalina.

I remember the first time I got hives was after eating lox on a Sunday morning when I was in elementary school. I have never eaten lox since then.

But I don't remember any sexual experiences—mostly repression—I remember thinking the girls in junior high who went to make-out parties were dirty girls, and I remember Alan waiting up for me when I went out on a date—not father—I think I was afraid of sex and that is why I waited to have sex until I got married. I don't know why I would have been afraid of doing it, except that it was forbidden according to the rules in the house.

I remember daddy having a terrible temper and being afraid of his temper.

I remember that the family hardly ever went on family vacations because it was hard to imagine all of us happily together for a long period of time, because our parents felt vacations were not important, but rather a pastime for families who were wealthier than we were. I do remember going to a ranch in Palm Springs where my father's friend had a vacation home.

I also remember going to Bass Lake and mother being terrified of father's drunk driving on the way back through Tioga Pass.

I think my mother stayed with my father because being the victim was the only role she knew how to act out. I think my separation from you and from mother had to do with not becoming a mother and avoiding the victimization that I saw trapping everyone in our family.

Most powerfully, I remember that I really didn't like my father very much at all; he was cruel to mother because he kept her frightened by his temper and we were all happier when he was gone; also I thought he was mean to Alan because he provoked Alan to get upset when he asked pedestrian questions which he knew would upset Alan. It didn't seem like he wanted to really understand anyone's feelings in the family at all. I don't think he was really any meaner to you than Alan or me, I just think you stood up to him and demanded things from him and mother which he wasn't willing to give you; if he had not been so selfish he would have tried to understand why you wanted things of him, why you deserved some help with your life; instead you became the extravagant twin and I withdrew into my world of books because they brought me wisdom and solace and my family didn't—except that I always loved you and loved to be with you—and it was hard for me when people criticized you for being overemotional, as I felt you were fine as you were and I guess I secretly hoped in a perfect world that mother and father would try to understand you; instead they labeled you.

I see you as the mother-sister because you are always more likely to worry about me.

I feel that it was daddy who was so cruel, more so than Alan, who I also see as a victim of father's jealousy and mother's revenge on father.

I like having you as my big sister. I like you just the way you are.

Love,

Marjorie

*   *   *

My sister's thoughts confirm my sensibilities, and even though we both believe she was not herself sexually victimized, she has suffered with me. We carried the pain of my secrets with us, which alienated us from each other.

I have come to understand my twin sister's feelings of shame and even her terror of being seen to be like me. Her feelings make sense to me because on some level, she knew about the incest but was unable to speak about it with me. The truth was too painful for her to accept. For many, many years my sister lived in exile, without the comfort of being my twin, because our shame was too overwhelming and the secret buried so deeply. Clearly she shared my secret, which terrified and isolated her from me. The family secret served to separate her from the closeness that we as twins share. Marjorie is also my secret sister.

I am aware that I have many secret sisters. Sexual abuse is a legacy that is handed down through generations. It is only recently that survivors of sexual abuse, researchers, and clinicians interested in understanding this traumatic injury have been able to talk openly about the pervasiveness of the problem as well as develop hopes for understanding how to cure this type of personal violation.

So many theories have shed light on why sexual abuse has been left a misunderstood and taboo subject throughout history and in our contemporary society. My understanding comes from my own personal and professional experiences as a secret sister to other women who survive in one way or another. The shame related to sexual abuse is intense and hidden. I have come to profoundly understand the insidious fear and disavowal and denial related to sexual abuse because I am a clinician who is also a survivor. I believe that understanding not only the shame but also the secrecy and sense of being damaged or defective is the key to helping victims reclaim their sense of dignity, entitlement, and value as unique individuals.

TEN

Treatment Issues with Survivors of Sexual Abuse

When I left my first analytic experience, I felt traumatized, betrayed, depressed, yet totally driven to perform for others. I didn't really understand what had happened to me in analysis. I had, in a manner of speaking, gotten worse, because there was no time for happiness or inner peace. I felt disconnected from my past and my present relationships. I looked good on paper, but I still felt bad about myself. The analysis had recreated emotionally the traumatic state of sexual abuse. My shame was suffocating me.

Specifically, the analysis was a failure for many reasons. First, it was a superficial therapeutic experience because I felt connected to Dr. Z in an unhealthy way. Was Dr. Z just superficial? Or was I just so terribly compliant that it was impossible to go beyond my hunger for accomplishment? I think that there is a frightening amount of truth to the interpretation that Dr. Z wasn't concerned enough with deep issues, while I was too afraid to do anything but listen to him give me prescriptions and directions. My problem was understandable. Dr. Z's mistake was unfortunate and negligent. I accumulated credentials and degrees to bolster my self-esteem as well as his self-confidence as an analyst, which masked the failure of the analysis. But there were other problems as well.

Certainly, and without a doubt, Dr Z and I were both victims of our times. Analysts in the 1970s thought that issues of sexuality were related to fantasies of an Oedipal origin. The occurrence of sexual abuse was in some ways a secret that the analytic community was not interested in exploring in any organized way. Analysts did not tend to believe that their patients were sexually abused unless they were totally disorganized, had vivid memories of their violent experiences, and needed hospitalization. Zelda Fitzgerald was the typical victim of sexual abuse who was locked up and left to decompensate and to die in a sanitorium. Sybil and her dozens of personalities is another example of what was thought to be a typical victim of incest.

Dr. Z was just another 1970s analyst who was not alert to the presence of sexual abuse in a conventional family setting. *Besides, I had no memories.* I had no reason to believe that I was a victim. I was from an upstanding Jewish family that valued education, achievement, and humanitarian efforts. Sexual abuse was supposedly *not* a common occurrence in a family like ours. I had no information, no insight, that would have led me to wonder about my relationship with my father and my brother. I did not believe that incest was something that could happen in my family. Dr. Z and I entered our therapeutic relationship in ignorance about the insidious nature of incest, which was understandable given the taboos our society held on to in the 1970s.

Dr. Z was also very invested in making interpretations and giving insights based on his theories about what underlying issues were causing what behavior. For example, I was the bad twin and my sister was the good twin because our "borderline mother" split us into the good part of herself and the bad part of herself. This inaccurate interpretation was the core organizing principle of all his other interpretations. In other words, classical analysis approached the patient by focusing on intellectual understanding and then making judgments based on beliefs about how the individual functioned and why, given the home environment and the family dynamics. Sometimes analysts thought about the genetic transmission of mental disease, but only if nothing else worked. The patient's feelings were not the focus of analytic work; rather, the patient's capacity to function was evaluated based on the analyst's judgments about what was adaptive and what was dysfunctional. Classical analysts knew what was right for the patient and what was wrong. They were objective, neutral, and in charge. They did not accept responsibility for therapeutic ruptures from mistakes or misattunements, as some analysts do in the 1990s. If your patient didn't get along with your treatment plan, then he or she was *resistant*—a pejorative term for being either uncooperative and/or untreatable. The analyst was rarely at fault. Any problem in the flow of therapy was always seen as being with the patient who was untreatable.

My personality structure, or who I was emotionally, was entirely vulnerable to being exploited by the classical analytic method, which was judgmental and authoritarian. I was compliant and cooperative because I got this message about how I should behave from Dr. Z, which was an exact recreation of my childhood experiences. I was afraid to talk back and complain. I was not a bully by nature who could say, "You're wrong" or "You're crazy." (I have patients that can do this to me naturally, and I think in some ways that they are less vulnerable to exploitation.) I didn't have a typical trust disorder that many survivors of sexual abuse have because I was a twin who overvalued intimacy. I craved talking and feeling connected. I feared abandonment because I got hurt when my sister abandoned me. I was hungry for the attention that came from intimacy.

I was not your typical incest victim who falls into the categories described in the current literature and research on sexual abuse. I had no trepidation about analysis. I wanted to understand my nightmares. Concerned with insight, I was capable of introspection. I was also intellectually inclined, though inhibited, and I always wanted to feel in control.

So my personality, the classic analytic method, and the climate of the 1970s with its taboos on incest worked against my getting help. But I think there were more serious problems that led to my sense of betrayal and my ultimate feeling of being victimized by Dr. Z. I believe that another therapist who was more aware and more interested in his or her own strengths and limitations might have gotten deeper into my childhood trauma. I believe that had Dr. Z been more interested in understanding me, we could have gotten further beyond his destructive interpretation about a good and a bad twin.

After many years of analysis and self-reflection, my conclusion is that Dr. Z was afraid of his own feelings, which made him afraid of the intensity of my feelings. His tendency toward emotional constriction based on his childhood, coupled with my tendency to withdraw, created a *therapeutic impasse*, which became the core problem of our work together. Dr. Z wanted to translate my passion and creativity into scholarship or art because it was easier for him to think about my life in that way. Trying to understand the intensity of my feelings was too painful for him. A therapist must feel comfortable with his or her feelings, as well as the patient's, as the literature on survivors of sexual abuse suggests that the intensity of affects is a symptom of traumatic abuse. For Dr. Z, my intensity was something to control, sublimate, or eradicate; understanding my pain was too difficult and too provocative for him.

I obviously cannot recommend the classical psychoanalytic method to incest survivors because it is judgmental, authoritarian, and self-serving at its worst. At best, it also seems outdated and obscure, remote and uncaring.

In contrast, Dr. Ace, who had been a classical analyst for many years, has been able to help me. He is a reformed, iconoclastic self-psychologist as well as a kind and caring human being who has been interested in my passion and intensity. Our work centered around developing psychic structure through affect attunement. More simply stated, my feelings were mirrored and valued to foster a more complete sense of myself. Dr. Ace's focus was not on the *interpretation* of my psychological history, as it was played out in the 1990s. Rather, he was concerned with how I was *feeling* about myself and about my relationship with him or with my relationships to significant others—namely, my husband, my children, my mother, and my twin sister. His focus from the beginning was on what I wanted from the situation. "I" was the focus of our work. There was no hidden agenda about how damaged I was. There was no room for exploitation. Dr. Ace built our relationship on his understanding of my different and fluctuating feeling states. He worked very hard to focus on my feelings, which were a serious problem for me and for him. I had too much training with Dr. Z, which led me to intellectualize and theorize about my life, rather than talking about my emotional experiences.

Dr. Ace was also very open-minded and protective, as well as supportive of my feelings. My feelings and reactions were of tantamount importance, and we need to understand them. I was not labeled or judged. Dr. Ace would always say to me, in response to my diagnostic-like self-criticism, "Why do you have to do that to yourself? Why give yourself a label?" His implication was that I was a real person with feelings and experiences, who was in pain. I was not a cluster of symptoms with a diagnostic label. I was always an individual who was in pain for reasons embedded in the present and the past. I was always treated with dignity. In this I have been very fortunate, for being treated with dignity and concern was an essential element in the recovery of my forgotten memories and my enhanced sense of self.

* * *

In looking back and reflecting on my treatment, as well as reading a great deal of current research on treating victims of incest or sexual abuse (see Selected References), I can see specific ways in which my second analysis was helpful, ways that might be generalizable to other victims of sexual abuse. As other researchers concur, treating the victim of sexual abuse can present its own particular problems. Specific aspects of my treatment were effective, and I believe they would be useful to other therapists working with victims and survivors of sexual abuse. I have used the ideas discussed below in my own work with my clients.

Hopefulness

From the onset of my treatment Dr. Ace was hopeful that we could understand my shame, depression, symptoms of forgetting, and multiple inhibitions. In spite of my strong and persistent transference distortions, my feeling that Dr. Ace was angry with me or that I was worthless, Dr. Ace became a new self object or parental figure for me. I never felt he ever saw me as untreatable or damaged. His interest was in the interpersonal experiences that caused me intense pain. I felt he was always focused on my sense of entitlement, especially my feelings.

I have been successful in working with my clients who are survivors of sexual abuse because I acknowledge that they are traumatized and afraid but not damaged irrevocably because of the violations to the cohesiveness of their self. I see my clients as injured by an unfair and unwarranted intrusiveness that they never asked for or expected. I try to dignify their pain and feel compassion for their emotional distress or symptoms.

Focus on Intensity of Affect Life

From our very first encounter until the termination of treatment, Dr. Ace was concerned with my fluctuating feeling states and what intensified or diminished my reactivity to people and situations. There was no evaluation of too much intensity or a lack of affect and/or lack of concentration or focus. My different feelings and alternating states of mind were merely reflected back to me within a framework that evolved from our dialogue. This process gradually led me back to my forgotten memories.

I try to use Dr. Ace's framework and style when I work with my own patients, focusing on my patients' feelings and body sensations that might indicate forgotten memories.

Focus on Transference Distortions

My serious problems with self-loathing and shame were re-
solved through transference interpretations. I became aware that
I felt judged by Dr. Ace and that this was my own projection.
He did not judge me. As he often said, "I know how I am feeling.
I'm not angry with you!" I tended to believe he was angry and
disappointed with me. These displaced feelings from my father
and brother were analyzed and understood as determinants of
childhood abuse and my previously endured traumatic life
situations.

Focusing on the transference distortions has been useful in
my work with patients who are able to work analytically. However, not all patients are able to work in an analytic mode. I
have found that *forcing* the analytic technique on patients is
alienating to the therapeutic bonding process and to the progress
of therapy.

Empathic Attunement

Dr. Ace was in almost every instance concerned with understanding how I was feeling. But he is human and did, naturally,
make some mistakes in understanding my subjective experiences. However, he maintained a sense of my pain and did not
become overidentified with either the pain or my despair. He
was able to tolerate my painful states of mind and not worry
about my well-being. He was protective, but not overprotective.
For example, he took a strong stand about the importance of
retrieving my memories. He believed I would remember what
I could tolerate remembering. He never *forced* me or *pushed* me
to remember. He concentrated on what my feelings would allow
me to process. He was not invested in my remembering every
detail I could as a measure of success in my treatment.

In working with my own patients, I find that some women
are interested in recovering memories of the abuse they experienced and others find it too painful. My experience has led me

to believe that pushing the patient to confront the past is not therapeutic. The patient must want to, and be able to, tolerate these intense affect states. I have heard horror stories about women who were forced to remember through hypnosis events that were still too intensely painful to integrate into their current experiences. Because of an overemphasis on remembering through hypnosis, patients can regress to painful psychotic states, which are not *curative*, just overwhelming or even psychically fragmenting and damaging.

Equal Partnership

From the beginning of therapy I felt that there was a mutuality to our work together. Dr. Ace did not profess to know the answers to my questions and fears. Rather, he focused on information to which I might be able to associate, which would help us understand more deeply the core issues of treatment. This approach encouraged me to associate to my own dreams. Ace considered his interpretations of my dreams as a distancing mechanism that would cover up important feelings and memories. He never said, "This means . . . " Instead, he asked, "What do you think this dream suggests?"

When I work with survivors of sexual abuse, I am careful to stay with their feelings and associations. I do *not* think that I know what will help them feel better about themselves. I do encourage my patients to focus on protecting themselves from being victimized again.

The Bond

Because Dr. Ace and I were equal partners in exploring the recesses of my past psychic life, disruptions in the bonding process were inevitable. Working through and understanding disruptions in our bond enhanced genuine intimacy and understanding. I'm sure that it is more difficult for me to come up with a specific example of misattunement and reparation of the bond than it would be for Dr. Ace. It really wasn't my work to stay connected. It was his job. So it is more difficult for me to describe how he managed to work through disharmony. There is one blatant example, I remember, which was not really reminiscent of our work together. This incident is funny now and illustrative of the bonding process. During my second or third year of analysis, I was lying on Dr. Ace's couch and having difficulty remembering the details of an experience crucial to my analysis. I was, of course, having trouble explaining my state of mind. He directed, "Can you try to just stay with that idea and give me your associations?" I retorted, with intense anger, "You are just such a mother-fucker from hell—stop pushing me." We tried to end the session calmly, but I remained upset. The next day, of course, I mentioned his lack of empathy and my reaction. His reply was funny. He told me that he had been called lots of different names in his long life as an analyst, but that I was the first person in his long and illustrious career to call him a "mother-fucker from hell." He was pleased that I felt some conviction about being angry at him and that I had expressed my feelings directly. This openness made our relationship stronger.

I believe that the bond established between me and my patients is what is ultimately the most curative aspect of treatment. My experience is that the bonding process with survivors of sexual abuse is particularly important and intimate. Victims and survivors are very sensitive to how others react to them. They yearn for more intense attachments. In addition, because of their traumatic experiences, when they do enter an intense relationship, they feel violated or hurt more easily than other patients.

Dignity

That my analyst focused on my feelings about what had happened to me without labeling them was extremely important. He always viewed my feelings as *valuable*. I never felt objectified by my analyst.

The issue of dignity is central with survivors of childhood trauma because they feel so intensely ashamed and humiliated. Any type of objectification of their problems or labeling or stereotyping of their experiences is not therapeutic. Objectification of experiences or labeling may lead to a disruption in the bond between patient and therapist and to further repression and false-self interactions between the patient and the therapist.

Protection

The issue of protection was very important for me. Doctor Z gave me a sense of protection by predicting or prescribing things to me. This turned out to be a false sense of protection. On the other hand, Ace was very careful not to make predictions or prescriptions for me. By focusing on my feelings, I was able to feel protected by him. In other words, because he often took my feelings more seriously than I did, he was able to establish a sense of safety so important to establishing a profound sense of trust in the process of my analysis. For example, if I said, "I am afraid to stay alone in that hotel room," he would respond, "Then trust your feelings and don't do it. You know what is best for yourself. If only you would trust your inclinations." He never said, "I don't think that you should do that," as Dr. Z had done all too many times.

I find that as a clinician I am very careful myself about giving my patients the message that they are fragile and in need of advice on how to run their lives. I try to help them come to their own conclusions about what might make them feel safer and more self-confident. This is something Dr. Z never fostered in me.

*   *   *

My treatment proceeded in a natural fashion, it *unfolded*, and it was successful. However, and interestingly enough, my treatment was also similar to case histories I have read about and listened to at conferences. This leads me to suggest that there are five phases of treatment common to survivors of incest or sexual abuse. They are outlined below.

Phase One: The Toleration of Affect

The initial work of psychotherapy is to establish a bond with the patient, which is based on the therapist's understanding of the patient's feeling states. Dr. Ace's dealing directly with my feeling states and the intensity of my affects, including my bodily sensations, was crucial. His sensitivity allowed me to trust him as a new self object or parental figure who could accept and tolerate who I was emotionally. This attunement was crucial in lessening my pervasive sense of shame.

Oftentimes it is very difficult for therapists to tolerate the affects of survivors of sexual abuse because their feelings may be too overwhelming to tolerate even for the therapists themselves. Incest survivors, intensely sensitive to others, often sense the therapist's capacity or incapacity to tolerate their feeling states. This monitoring system, already in place from childhood, unconsciously influences the patient to tell the therapist only what is acceptable. *Therapists need to understand their countertransference feelings.* If the therapist feels revolted, overstimulated, or overwhelmed by the patient, then they will be unable to work together.

Dr. Ace encouraged me to know my feelings and my inclinations. He encouraged me to talk about my emotional pain. He was not frightened or repulsed by my feelings and experiences. On the other hand, neither was he remote or removed from my trauma. I experienced him as separate from me but still emotionally available for me. This is a difficult position to take when dealing with traumatic emotional illnesses. Often the therapist becomes overidentified with the patient's pain or is revolted by the patient's experiences. Dr. Ace was able to maintain compassion for me. He was hopeful that I could also feel compassionate for myself. In this way he helped me to retrieve my forgotten memories, those remembrances that because of their intense pain had remained buried for so many years.

This focus on the acceptance of feeling states, including memory fragments and body pain, was the first step in our work and a thread that ran through the entire analysis. I believe that focusing on what the patient brings to the therapeutic session is the initial phase of working with survivors of sexual abuse. In addition, a lack of memories is a signal to me that there is a possibility of sexual abuse.

Phase Two: Reduction of Stress

A common personality characteristic of survivors of sexual abuse is an overzealous need to accomplish too many unrealistic goals in order to defend against their deep sense of defectiveness, their ensuing depression, and a need to feel in control. Dr. Ace worked very hard with me to help me reduce some of my overdetermined and compulsive need for overachievement in order to reduce the number of stressful situations in my life, which often left me feeling overwhelmed and burdened. By reducing stress in my life, I was able to focus on more internal issues.

The reduction of stress is essential for all survivors in treatment. Overachievement, eating disorders, drug abuse, alcohol problems, and sexual promiscuity are all used to mask the horrible sense of defectiveness and other overwhelming feelings of incest victims. Understanding how food, drugs, alcohol, and sex are used to tolerate pain is necessary if such use is to be reduced.

Phase Three: Uncovering Forgotten Memories

With a firm connection to my analyst and a lifestyle more contained and supportive of my idiosyncrasies, I was able to begin to retrieve memories of my past. The task of confronting my pervasive early childhood amnesia for in-house experiences, dissociation experiences, and memory lapses was tedious and required a great deal of focus on painful states. The survivor needs to be able to deal with serious traumatic problems exclusively for a long period of time.

I find that when I work with patients, both of us need a strong commitment to the therapeutic process in order to recover forgotten memories that have been repressed. This type of connection between therapist and patient is not always possible, as the arousal of shame and intense pain can often feel totally consuming and overwhelming for the patient and the therapist both.

Phase Four: Confrontation

It was important in my experience to try to confront people in my past who might be able to help remember what had happened. Confrontation with other people, whether supportive or nonsupportive, helps reduce overwhelming feelings of shame and increases a sense of entitlement. Speaking up about the past also allows the incest survivor to develop a support network outside of psychotherapy.

I find that confrontation with significant others in the survivor's past is necessary if the patient is going to feel better about him or herself in a lasting way. A group support system is also very useful to help survivors accept the importance of their own painful experiences, for others view them as important also.

Phase Five: Integrating the Trauma

Working through traumatic experiences from the past occurs during the last phase of treatment. The survivor needs to learn to deal with the world from a position of power, rather than helplessness. This capacity to deal with others assertively is the last phase of treatment and may continue as long as the patient feels vulnerable. Although I believe that it is difficult to forget what has gone before that has been traumatic, I know that old demons gradually seem less scary and more manageable.

*   *   *

Dr. Ace wrote the following summary about my treatment.

October 15, 1992

Dr. Schave has asked me to write a brief description of my understanding of the nature and vicissitudes of her psychological pain for the purpose and clarification for her editors of her forthcoming book:

Relatively early in our work, I came to understand her pain as derived from her personality organization. She seemed to be organized on the basic principle that her very existence depended on how successful she was in putting herself at the disposal of others. This means total mental attention to her perception of significant others' changing needs and pleasures, with total inattention to her own needs, feelings, and inclinations: a life of painful slavery with the ever-present danger of banishment and annihilation if she didn't do well enough. I am speaking of her definition of her own identity and required role in life. How this psychological organization developed, what early experiences fed into the development of this life view, is another matter, beyond the purpose of these notes.

These words clarify for me the nature of her ever-present psychological pain, always afraid of not doing well enough for the other, and risking annihilation or the alternative of rebelling and suffering the pain of loneliness and isolation.

She did demonstrate that she had several refuges from pain—all inefficient and costing a high price. I will try to describe three: disassociation, achievement, and amnesia. Early in life, she developed the ability to disassociate herself from the experience of pain—by viewing the situation intellectually, rather than experiencing it. This cost her the tendency to become more and more cut off from her feelings. Thus, this primary need to please the significant other enough in quantity and quality. This mechanism, despite her unusual productivity, offered her only brief relief before the doubts about whether she had done well enough crept in and resumed her torment. Understandably, this also left her in a chronic state of fatigue and with the burden of what was still to be done to earn acceptance.

Achievement: Her natural talents led her to superior academic achievement early, and later as a clinical psychologist and author. But usual accompanying and stimulating feelings of mastery, enhanced self-worth, and pleasure were mild and brief or sometimes completely absent. Instead she was plagued by the question of whether she was doing well enough in quantity and quality to please the other, enough to stave off destruction for another day. In brief, acheivement was accompanied by a transient good feeling followed by long painful anxiety and terror.

Disassociation: Early in life she developed the ability to disassociate her painful emotional reaction in a situation from the event by viewing herself in the situation from without—this helped her disassociate herself and her feelings from the traumatic event. It successfully relieved pain at a high price, namely, becoming detached from her own feeling life, and ultimately led to a deadened existence.

Amnesia: She developed amnesia for large blocks of her childhood, with only isolated innocuous memories surviving. Forgetting the traumatic events protected her from the pain of reexperiencing the painful attendant feelings. Again, the price was pain of another sort: feeling ashamed that her secret, kept even from herself, must be horrible; and in addition, maybe she was even responsible for the events. She lived with the conscious private pain that she embodied a terrible secret whose dimensions she did not know.

In considering how to describe the treatment of Dr. Schave from my point of view, I have decided to divide it into phases, somewhat artificial and oversimplified, but I can't think of a better way in a brief description.

With her personality organization, I am sure you will anticipate that in the first stage of treatment it was necessary to address her theories about my motive for taking her as a patient. They all had one common thread: She had to make the experience nice for me, interesting for me, and not stressful for me. Although this was in the foreground in the beginning, this took a long time to die. Finally, she seriously considered that I didn't require her to devote herself totally to my comfort. Then she needed a considerable period of time to trust that getting reacquainted with her own feelings and inclinations was safe. There was a period of pleasant anticipation mixed with apprehension about the forbidden and unknown.

The pain of this period can be understood as her being encouraged to trust a new view of herself and the world—as possibly without risking annihilation. Finally, she tentatively and apprehensively experimented with a new, inner-directed life experience where she was motivated by her inner personal, unique interests and inclinations rather than the previous almost complete focus on what the other needed and wanted. Again, this stimulated feelings of excitement and feelings of an unknown dread. The dread, of course, was due to the variance in behavior with her lifelong pattern and the inability to completely trust that it was safe to change. Now, when she did act in the other's behalf, her motivation was her own caring, compassion, and understanding, rather than from outside pressure and outside need.

During this phase, as she experimented with a new life view, she repeatedly experienced pain-free periods of longer and longer duration. When the pain returned, she could be helped to recover her pain-free state quickly by bringing her attention again to her own feelings and inclinations and point of view. It was at this time that she first mentioned her inclination to write a book about her own experience.

In the termination phase of our work, the old tendency reasserted itself but was easily put to rest as she continued to feel better. Characteristically, she rushed herself toward termination for my benefit. When she recognized this tendency, it was easy to again respect her own inclinations and wait until it felt right to her to end the treatment.

In closing, I have a need to remind you that my description of Dr. Schave's pain and recovery comes from my own subjectivity, retrospection, and reconstruction and is in no way objective reality. I truly believe that Dr. Schave is really the ultimate authority about descriptions of her pain as well as her healing.

*   *   *

I have been able to work with sexually abused patients because I can consciously and unconsciously identify with their shame.

In addition, I have a sense of hopefulness and compassion, which helps my patients to strive on, even when life and therapy feel overwhelming, bleak, and hopeless.

My ability to identify with a patient is useful to the progress of therapy. For example, I remember my first clinical experience as a trainee at Camarillo State Hospital (CSH). A young woman who had been seriously sexually abused by her stepfather was suffering from multiple personalities, which in the 1980s was a misunderstood diagnosis. I was, so to speak, the new kid on the staff, and this young woman was my first patient but somehow I was able to work with her. She made a strong attachment to me, even when she was changing personalities. I, in turn, was very concerned about helping her. I had, truly, the finest and most experienced supervisors of psychotic illness, and even they were amazed at my intuitive sense of how to work with this young woman. I remember speaking at "grand rounds" to the entire hospital about the case and getting the go-ahead to follow my sense of how to work therapeutically with this young woman.

I saw Becky and her 12 personalities three times a week in analytic therapy for nine months. She was able to leave the hospital and return to her board and care. She writes to me now to tell me how she is doing on her own.

Some of the staff at CSH thought that Becky would quickly return to the hospital. Others thought that I was a weird but clinically gifted genius. I know, however, that it was my ability to connect unconsciously with her pain that allowed me to help her begin to recover some of her strengths to face the world. I cannot exactly remember and then analyze what I did and said, for she was literally my first patient. I now remember that when she slit her wrists or changed personalities in front of me, I was not afraid that she was untreatable. I wanted to help her out of that horrible hospital. I won the battle.

I have also worked extensively with Lori, my young actress patient, who was sexually abused by her father and emotionally tormented by her mother's ambivalence about her painful experiences and her memories. Lori has been made to feel like a liar or someone just not strong enough to take what life had given her when in fact she was seriously abused. She has given up hope for reconciliation with her father, but her mother remains connected to Lori through her own guilt and shame and a wish to change Lori's mind for her own peace of mind. Perhaps her mother's childish attitude will change, although the prospect is bleak, given Lori's mother's network of friends.

Along the road of my clinical experiences I have met other women and men who were sexually abused and who have developed differing symptoms, from high overachievers to recovering alcoholics and to drug users. Some individuals know they are victims of incest or sexual abuse, but they cannot deal with what has happened to them. They really can't bear to break down their defenses and work on their hidden terror and sadness. Other victims have put their secrets about being sexually abused aside in a box that is buried under success and the "good things" in life.

I have worked with many children who seem to be able to openly confront their own confusion related to being violated sexually. It is most often the shame of the parents that makes the children's problems with self-loathing even more serious.

* * *

Surrendering to understanding the trauma of sexual abuse takes a great deal of courage by both therapist and patient. Therapists need to have the tenacity, insight, and self-understanding to deal with the hidden, scary issues and the intense affects that these issues arouse. Patients need to give another individual the trust that was destroyed by the violations of their ego boundaries when they were abused. This is a difficult yet worthwhile journey.

Afterword

Marjorie Title Ford

"It doesn't happen all at once," said the skin horse. "You become. It takes a long time. That's why it doesn't often happen to people who break easily, or have sharp edges, or who have to be carefully kept. Generally, by the time you are Real, most of your hair has been loved off, and your eyes drop out and you get loose in the joints and very shabby. But these things don't matter at all, because once you are real, you can't be ugly, except to people who don't understand."

From *The Velveteen Rabbit* by Margery Williams

Reading and reflecting on this manuscript makes me feel like there is still much to be uncovered and shared about the impact of sexual abuse on the human spirit. I remember a conversation Barbara and I had several months after our reconciliation, during the last months of Mother's life. We were on a long walk; Barbara was trying to explain to me about how she felt when she and Douglas took Mother to the psychiatrist to try to help her overcome the depression that was killing her. Barbara shared with me what it was like for her to hear Mother reveal the pain of her relationship with Father, his abuse, and the reality that she had been abused as a child. I was trying to accept the reality that both Mother and Barbara had been abused. I was beginning to feel that I, too, have forgotten memories.

Then suddenly my deep interest in Virginia Woolf's life made more sense to me. I realized at that moment that my fascination with Virginia Woolf's struggle with depression and insanity was a way I was trying to understand my family's emotional suffering. Starting at eighteen, I began reading the biographies of Virginia Woolf after being introduced to her novels in an English course. These biographies were fascinating, but never totally satisfying to me. I wanted to understand why Woolf's depression led her to periods of despair, psychosis, and attempted suicide. I wanted to understand why such a brilliant woman could be a victim. I wanted to understand why she had suffered so and could still give the world so much insight into the role of women and mothers in the psychic life of our civilization.

I had always looked to and continue to explore Woolf's writing for solace. Even before the many biographies that acknowledge Virginia Woolf was sexually abused and psychologically damaged, I knew unconsciously and intuitively that Woolf had experienced something that other writers could not express in their writing that I could identify with and understand. As Woolf's autobiographical writing, some of which was written only months before her suicide in 1941, began to be taken more seriously, female biographers began to emphasize the devastating impact of Woolf's sexual abuse and victimization by her stepbrothers from the time Woolf was eight years old and throughout her adolescence. I remember first reading Phyllis Rose's biography of Woolf and then Lyndal Gordon's. Both biographers saw Woolf's abuse as crucial determinants of her depression and psychotic despair. In 1989, fifteen years after I had started trying to understand Virginia Woolf's life, Louise De Salvo's biography, *Virginia Woolf: The Impact of Childhood Sexual Abuse on Her Life and Work*, was published. This biography argues that Woolf's sexual victimization as a child was the most important factor in her psychological instability and depression. During my walk with Barbara, I realized how the publication of De Salvo's biography was an important key to understanding our past.

Because of the deepening and growing interest in feminism that began in the mid-1960s, which encouraged more women to study and practice psychology, the extensive and destructive impact of childhood sexual abuse has been presented to the public through literature and psychological texts. What was ignored or underemphasized by earlier writers such as Julian Bell has finally been dramatically illustrated by De Salvo and others. Now I too can connect more with my past through Virginia Woolf. Again, as I see it now, I read Woolf because I knew we had lived through similar family situations. Although this realization is speculative and subjective, it makes sense to Barbara and to me.

I am deeply interested in the relationship between pain and creative expression. I feel tremendously proud of my sister who has unmasked her own suffering and who has helped others to overcome their pain both as a therapist and as a writer. Reading of Barbara's experience with the patients she has helped reminds me of how complex, sensitive, and strong Barbara is as a human being; to say that her suffering has not been in vain is to intellectualize the years of depression and estrangement that both of us have lived through. I believe in the power of her journey. She has turned her pain into a gift of giving and helping others. There is no greater gift; no gift is more meaningful.

My sister's book and her story are helping me to face my own pain; sometimes I feel miles behind her. In spite of all I have accomplished, I know how low my self-esteem is, yet I know that she is helping me to face whatever it is in me that makes me feel so worthless. I cherish my relationship with Barbara, a relationship that was dormant for so many years.

I still fear failing Barbara; I don't know if I am a coward deep in my soul, or if it was all of the years that we fought because people pitted us against one another, comparing and contrasting us ruthlessly. The legacy of having to be perfect, of having to be good, follows me wherever I go. My fear of failing her is vivid. What failure could be worse? I remember how fragile our relationship can feel.

Although it was almost a year ago, I think about the time when I tried to help Barbara with matters related to Alan and our trust as if it were yesterday. I was unsuccessful; Mother could still not acknowledge Alan's selfishness openly through amending her will. Barbara was overwhelmed by Alan's self-centered arrogance that had trapped us for so many years. Barbara got angry at me that day. We didn't speak for almost two weeks, and my depression was unbearable. Finally I called her, and her husband answered. An analyst himself, Douglas kept me on the phone and reminded me that I had played the game of footsie with Alan and Barbara as a child and that I was a part of what had happened between them. I felt hurt by his words, but I waited for Barbara to come and talk to me. Then we reconnected. I hope to overcome my fear of her rejection of me and my fear of failing her and her family one day. I know that the love I feel for my sister, brother-in-law, niece, nephew, and for my own children and husband is rooted in the love that my mother gave to both Barbara and me. I believe that Mother did the very best she could; if she had been raised in a healthy home, she would still have been a remarkable woman and a wonderful mother. When I think about the circumstances of her life, that she was a victim as a child and as a wife, her courage to love us seems even more powerful and more radiant.

Forgotten Memories gives me courage to face my pain; I know that my sister's words and story will also give you courage to look within yourself, to begin the difficult process of understanding and unmasking your painful memories. I often think about the children's story *The Velveteen Rabbit* by Margery Williams about the stuffed rabbit who is tattered and dirty and fears being discarded. The toy rabbit magically becomes Real when he realizes that he is genuinely loved by the little boy with whom he stayed during a serious illness. I believe that all of us become real once we know that we are loved, even if we are imperfect, bruised, or disfigured. We are real when we can finally accept ourselves and when we know that we are loved for who we really are.

Selected References

Bass, E., and L. Davis. 1988. *The Courage to Heal*. New York: Harper & Row.

Blume, S. 1989. *Secret Survivors*. New York: John Wiley.

Courtois, C. 1988. *Healing the Incest Wound*. New York: W.W. Norton.

Dewald, P. 1989. "Effects on an Adult of Incest in Childhood: A Case Report." *Journal of Psychoanalysis*. Vol. 37, pp. 997–1015.

Finkelor, D. 1979. *Sexually Victimized Children*. New York: Free Press.

Finkelor, D. 1984. *Child Sexual Abuse: New Theory and Research*. New York: Free Press.

Frederickson, R. 1992. *Repressed Memories: A Journey to Recovery from Sexual Abuse*. New York: Simon & Schuster.

Freud, S. 1921. "Three Essays on the Theory of Sexuality." *Standard Edition of the Complete Psychological Works of Sigmund Freud*. Vol. 7. London: Hogarth Press.

Gelinas, D. 1983. "The Persisting Negative Effects of Incest." *Psychiatry*. Vol. 46, pp. 312–332.

Heiman, J., and E. Schatzaw. 1984. "Time-limited Group Therapy for Women with a History of Incest." *International Journal of Group Psychotherapy*. Vol. 34, No. 4, pp. 605–614.

Kohut, H. 1977. *The Restoration of the Self*. New York: International University Press.

Kohut, H. 1984. *How Does Analysis Cure?* Chicago: University of Chicago Press.

Levine, H. 1990. *Adult Analysis and Childhood Sexual Abuse*. Hillsdale, N.J.: Analytic Press.

Masson, J. 1984. *The Assault on the Truth: Freud's Suppression of the Seduction Theory*. New York: Farrar, Straus & Giroux.

Masson, J. 1991. *Final Analysis: The Making and Unmaking of a Psychoanalyst*. New York: Harper-Collins.

Meiselman, K. 1979. *Incest: A Psychological Study of Causes and Effects with Treatment Recommendation*. San Francisco: Jossey Bass.

Miller, A. 1981. *Prisoners of Childhood: The Drama of the Gifted Child and the Search for the True Self*. New York: Basic Books.

Miller, A. 1983. *For Your Own Good: Hidden Cruelty in Child-Rearing and the Roots of Violence*. New York: Farrar, Straus & Giroux.

Miller, A. 1984. *Thou Shalt Not Be Aware: Society's Betrayal of the Child*. New York: Farrar, Straus & Giroux.

Miller, A. 1988. *Banished Knowledge: Facing Childhood Injuries*. New York: Doubleday.

Nabokov, V. 1955. *Lolita*. New York: Putnam.

Noël, B., and K. Watterson. 1992. *You Must Be Dreaming*. New York: Poseidon Press.

Ornstein, A. 1974. "The Dread to Repeat and the New Beginning: A Contribution to the Psychoanalysis of the Narcissistic Personality Disorders." *Annual of Psychoanalysis*. Vol. 2, pp. 231–248.

Ornstein, A. 1981. "Self-Pathology in Childhood: Developmental and Clinical Considerations." *Psychiatric Clinics of North America*. Vol. 4, No. 3, pp. 435–453.

Ornstein, A., and P. Ornstein. 1980. "Parenting as a Function of the Adult Self: A Psychoanalytic Developmental Perspective." *Parental Influences: In Health and Disease*. Boston/Toronto: Little, Brown.

Perlman, S. 1992. "Psychoanalysis with Incest Survivors." Unpublished doctoral dissertation, Southern California Psychoanalytic Institute, Los Angeles.

Perlman, S. In press. "Unlocking Incest Memories: Pre-Oedipal Transference, Countertransference, and the Body." *Journal of the American Academy of Psychoanalysis*.

Schave, B. 1982. "Similarities and Differences in Six-year-old Identical and Fraternal Twins and Their Parents on Measures of Locus of Control and Normal Development." Unpublished Ed.D. doctoral dissertation, University of Southern California, Los Angeles.

Schave, B., and J. Ciriello. 1983. *Identity and Intimacy in Twins: A Developmental Perspective.* New York: Praeger.

Shane, E., and M. Shane. 1990. "The Opening Phase: A Developmental Perspective." In *On Beginning an Analysis,* edited by T. Jacobs and A. Rothstein. Madison, CT: International University Press.

Socarides, D., and R. Stolorow, 1984-85. "Affects and Selfobjects." *Annual of Psychoanalysis.* Vol. 12-13, pp. 105–119.

Stern, D. 1985. *The Interpersonal World of the Infant: A View from Psychoanalysis and Developmental Psychology.* New York: Basic Books.

Stoller, R. 1968. *Sex and Gender: On the Development of Masculinity and Femininity.* New York: Science House.

Stolorow, R., and G. Atwood. 1987. "From the Subjectivity of Science to the Science of Subjectivity." In *Theories of the Unconscious and Theories of the Self,* edited by R. Stern. Hillsdale, N.J.: Analytic Press.

Stolorow, R., and B. Brandchaft. 1988. "Developmental Failure and Psychic Conflict." *Psychoanalytic Psychology.* Vol. 3, No. 4, pp. 241–253.

"The Cutting Edge, 1992: Erotic Mysteries: Intimacy, Surreality and Gender in the 90's." Symposium, University of California, Department of Psychiatry, San Diego. San Diego: Info Media.

Ulman R., and D. Brothers. 1988. *The Shattered Self: A Psychoanalytic Study of Trauma.* Hillsdale, N.J.: Analytic Press.

Westerlund, E. 1992. *Women's Sexuality after Childhood Incest.* New York: W.W. Norton.

Wolf, E. 1988. *Treating the Self.* New York: Guilford Press.

Index

amnesia, 29–30; confronting, 46–47, 50, 56, 130–31; hypnosis and, 126; incest and, 107; phobias and, 66–67, 69, 87; recognition of, 33, 70, 124; as refuge from pain, 132, 133; shame and, 5, 133; as symptom of abuse, 130; symptoms of, 70; therapeutic bond and, 43; traumatic experiences and, 86–88

amnesia, recovery from, 1–2; desire for, 64–66, 68–69, 70; factors contributing to, 70; patient's feelings and, 125–26; physical reactions and, 63; self-perception and, 71–72, 90–91, 123; sister's account and, 114–18; toleration of, 89

analyst/therapist: abuse denial and, 96; abuse detection by, 63, 120; accountability and, 9; amnesia recovery and, 91; confronting, 45–46, 57, 59; countertransference by, 26, 28, 63, 84; misinterpretation by, 28, 76; necessity of, 107; objectivity and, 11–13; overidentification with, 21, 34, 37–38, 40; patient approach by, 8–10; patient compatibility with, 57, 58; patient dependence on, 8; recovering memories and, 130–31; and self-knowledge, 58; stress reduction and, 130; toleration of affect by, 129–30; training and, 8–9, 10; trust in, 42, 96, 129. *See also* patient victimization

anger: at analyst, 7, 62–64, 102–3, 127; of analyst, 34; objects of, 13–14; open discussions and, 105; at perpetrators, 101

Bell, Julian, 139
betrayal. *See* patient victimization

Camarillo State Hospital, 135
childhood sexual abuse: acceptance of experiencing, 86, 137; amnesia and, 29–30, 33; detection of, 3–4, 19, 46; gifted children and, x–xi; isolation and, ix–x; litigation and, 106–7; per-

About the Author

BARBARA SCHAVE is a practicing clinical psychologist in Beverly Hills. She is the author of four books in the areas of developmental psychology and education: *Identity and Intimacy in Twins* (Praeger, 1983), *Curriculum Design* (1984), *Issues in School Reform* (1985), and *Early Adolescence and the Search for Self* (Praeger, 1989). She works with survivors of sexual abuse in her clinical private practice.